MOTIVATING CLAS[...]

LB2013 G58[...]

P9-CJC-171

DATE DUE

NO 18 '94			
NO 17 '95			
JE 1 '95			
JY 27 '95			
JY 11 '96			
MAY 22 '97			
JY 1 '00			
JY 25 '01			
JE 11 '01			
NO 26 '01			
NV 22 '02			
JE 10 '02			
JE 3 '03			

Motivating Classroom Discipline

MOTIVATING CLASSROOM DISCIPLINE

William J. Gnagey

Illinois State University

UNIVERSITY
PRESS OF
AMERICA

AUG   '94

Lanham • New York • London

University Press of America®, Inc.

4720 Boston Way
Lanham, Maryland 20706

3 Henrietta Street
London WC2E 8LU England

All rights reserved
Printed in the United States of America
British Cataloging in Publication Information Available

This edition was reprinted in 1990 by arrangement with
Macmillan Publishing Company, New York, New York

Sincere Thanks Go To My Wife, Jill Walker Gnagey,
For Her Expert Help In Preparing The Manuscript

Library of Congress Cataloging-in-Publication Data

Gnagey, William J., 1927–   .
Motivating classroom discipline / William J. Gnagey.
p.   cm.
Reprint. First published: New York :
Macmillan Pub. Co., ©1981.
Includes bibliographical references (p.).
1. Classroom management.   2. Motivation in education.
3. School vandalism.   4. School violence.
5. Problem children—Discipline.   I. Title.
LB3013.G583   1990   371.1'024—dc20   89–28616 CIP

ISBN 0–8191–7663–X

The paper used in this publication meets the minimum requirements of
American National Standard for Information Sciences—Permanence
of Paper for Printed Library Materials, ANSI Z39.48–1984.

Preface

This *is not* a book on criminology. It does not purport to solve problems of murder, theft, assault, and drug abuse that just happen to take place on school property. As Doyle (1978) points out, to focus on juvenile crime would distort the true picture of school discipline, that hour-by-hour task of securing and maintaining the cooperation of students in classroom activities.

This book *does* attempt to bring together the colorful and exciting adventure of classroom teaching and the results of carefully planned educational research. Using a simplified model of human motivation, we have tied together the results of a large number of investigations into classroom discipline. We hope the resulting package will help teachers improve the effectiveness of their most crucial profession—educating tomorrow's citizens.

William J. Gnagey

Illinois State University
Normal, Illinois

Contents

One

Disruption in Algebra I: An Introduction

Mr. Linker had just left the room to answer an emergency telephone call in the principal's office. His freshman algebra class was supposed to be starting their next day's assignment. Although he hadn't had time to explain the lesson fully, he had instructed the group to get down to work while he was gone and warned them that there was to be no "funny business" while he was away.

Things went all right for nearly ten minutes. By this time about two-thirds of the class seemed to be hung up on problem three. There was some discussion about a new term, and several of the conscientious members of the class approached Ronald about the matter. Ronald, an A student, was already on number five and didn't want to be bothered. The buzzing increased in volume, and some giggling began in one corner.

It was at this point that Roscoe began his little act. Pulling his glasses down on his nose like the principal, Mr. Beggs, he began an artful and uproarious takeoff on a recent auditorium harangue that Mr. Beggs had made, concerning the proper clothing to be worn at Streamline High. The class was immediately convulsed and showed their appreciation with uncontrolled laughter and a few boos and catcalls. This response spurred Roscoe on to even greater heights.

No one knew how long Mr. Beggs had been peering through the window, but everyone knew Mr. Beggs was furious. Tight-lipped and white with anger, the principal intruded into the bedlam at the peak of Roscoe's mimicry. The program ground to an ominous halt.

The principal shoved Roscoe roughly against the front wall and began the inevitable reprimand. "I might have known it would be you, Roscoe," he seethed. "You've been accomplishing nothing but this asinine clowning ever since you came here. But this time you won't get away with it. Get down to my office and we'll see how funny you feel when your parents find out that you're expelled for a month."

Mr. Beggs thrust Roscoe toward the door and turned to glare at the class. "Since you all thought the little act was so funny, you can report to this room after school for a forty-minute detention period. Mr. Linker will be here to see that no more of this buffoonery goes on." This last pronouncement was shot at the returning algebra teacher, who had just reentered the room.

Mr. Beggs made a stormy exit, hauling the hapless Roscoe forcefully by one arm. Mr. Linker closed the door quietly as he tried to imagine how such a volcano could have erupted in fifteen short minutes.

HOW CAN YOU STOP A VOLCANO FROM ERUPTING?

It is the rare teacher who hasn't had something like this happen to his class. The names and faces may be different, but the plot is all too familiar. Somehow things get out of hand, and the roof blows off; you wonder how you ever got into such a fix.

It's enough of a disaster to your self-confidence when the explosion can be contained within your own classroom, but when your principal gets into the act, small feelings of anxiety begin to well up inside you. You know too well that more teachers are fired for their inability to keep discipline than for any other reason. Something has got to change!

The problem is deciding where to begin. Your college courses—what you can remember of them—all seem so general. There were no Roscoes or Ronalds or Mr. Beggses in the educational psychology text, but your instructor is certain to have made some pointed allegations about how most discipline problems are traceable to some weakness in the teaching. Your anxiety feelings begin to border on panic.

Program Effective Discipline

Perhaps in the year 2084 each college of education will present its fledgling teachers with the ultimate graduation gift, tiny fail-safe computers programmed to anticipate and solve all possible disciplinary problems that could arise in the classroom. Instead of pushing the panic button when pedagogical disaster threatens, the fearful amateur would merely enter the proper variables, press a function key, and follow the directions displayed on the tiny screen. With technology like that, Mr. Linker could have organized his Algebra I class so that the assignment would have been completed effectively in his absence, and principal Beggs might even be recommending him for a merit raise.

Understand Human Motivation

While we can't wait for such "Star Wars" developments to be realized, we can make use of some of the software components already available. It seem logical to assume that any such program would have to be based on some valid model of human behavior, with appropriate subroutines patterned after the results of educational research. For this book we have chosen a motivational model for the basic program. It is presented both verbally and graphically in Chapter 2, so that it can become an overall cognitive structure for predicting student behavior and misbehavior. Each of the succeeding chapters presents more specific examples of the dynamic interaction of needs, arousal, expectancy, reward, and punishment.

Avoid Ineffective Leadership

Chapter 3 describes three pathological teaching styles that exacerbate student misbehavior rather than avoid it. In attempting to fulfill their own needs, the despot, the flirt, and the nonentity misuse the elements of motivation in a most counterproductive way.

Be Sensitive to Outside Causes

Chapter 4 summarizes our knowledge about personal and social factors that predispose some students to misbehave more than others. An understanding of such outside causes may be essential for a teacher to make the most effective motivational moves in the classroom.

Make Effective Rules

Student motivation is strongly influenced by the way rules are made and enforced in the school. Chapter 5 explains some bases for classroom rules and details guidelines for composing and implementing an effective list.

Prevent Unnecessary Trouble

Knowing what motivational moves may prevent student misbehavior is a must for classroom teachers. Chapter 6 details a number of precautions that have proven to be effective in keeping many discipline problems from developing.

Use Antiseptic Control Techniques

Once misbehaviors have occurred, teachers must be skilled in taking measures that restore an effective learning situation. Chapter 7 describes specific techniques that terminate disruption without producing harmful side effects.

Teach Appropriate Behavior

Since school-appropriate behaviors must be taught, Chapter 8 describes specific moves that teachers can make to get the job done.

Techniques of behavior modification are presented along with proven methods of increasing pupil self-control.

Rewrite and Debug Your Program

It is our hope that this book will help you improve the discipline program that you now have in your memory tapes. Each chapter begins with a list of objectives that will alert you to the major points to be discussed. This list can also be used as brief essay questions with which to measure your own comprehension of the material after you have read it.

Each chapter ends with a feedback quiz, made up of a number of multiple-choice items that cover the same major points. Answer keys in the appendix (pp. 145–146) will help you make sure that the input has been complete and accurate.

But as you know, even the most experienced programmers must try out their creations using actual data. In your continued interaction with the Roscoes, Ronalds, and Mr. Beggses in your life, you will certainly find some changes and some additions that will make the suggestions in this text more effective for maintaining discipline in your own classes. Good luck!

Two

Achieving Classroom Discipline: A Motivation Model

OBJECTIVES

1. Define *motivation* and list five major forces that influence it.

2. Define *needs* and list seven categories described by Abraham Maslow.

3. Differentiate between maintenance and growth needs, according to Maslow's theory.

4. Explain why Maslow has arranged human needs in a hierarchy.

5. Explain the relationship between motivation and effective discipline.

6. Explain how the effective disciplinarian makes use of student needs.

7. Define *arousal* and list five forces that influence it.

8. Explain how the effective teacher uses arousal to maintain class discipline.

9. Define *expectancy* and list four forces that influence it.

10. Explain how teachers can use expectancy to maintain effective classroom discipline.

11. Define *reward* and explain how an effective teacher can reinforce appropriate behavior.

12. Define *punishment* and describe two different categories that may be used.

13. Explain how punishment can be used to decrease misbehavior and the potential danger in its overuse.

he succeeding chapters are full of specific, research-based suggestions about maintaining classroom discipline. Before we begin to describe these concrete manipulations, we would like to offer a general model of human motivation as a meaningful structure into which most of these diverse findings may be fit. It is our hope that a solid understanding of the principles that underlie disciplinary procedures will make it easier for you to transpose them into your own teaching situation and even to invent some new ones for yourself.

Let us think of *motivation* as the total of all the forces that cause a person to expend energy doing one thing rather than another. Let us say that *good discipline* refers to a situation in which your students are exerting an optimal amount of energy trying to learn what you want to teach them instead of wasting it in various other counter-productive activities. You can be called a *good disciplinarian* when you have learned to use the forces of motivation to keep your students moving toward their academic goals instead of misbehaving.

WHAT FORCES INFLUENCE MOTIVATION?

Figure 1 pictures the flower-shaped analog model we have designed to symbolize motivation. You will note that although human needs are

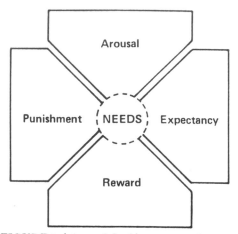

FIGURE 1 / A model of human motivation.

central to the process, arousal, expectancy, reward, and punishment are also influential in motivation. The dotted line between the needs and the other forces symbolizes their constant and dynamic interaction. Although we may choose to explicate them one by one, they seldom, if ever, operate in such isolation.

Needs Are Central

Students are always trying to fulfill their own *needs.* This is the principal reason that they act the way they do. Certain biological and psychological disequilibria cause them enough discomfort to trigger various responses calculated to banish those aversive feelings. Abraham Maslow (1954) has listed four classes of *maintenance needs* that recurrently press for reduction. As modified by Root (1970), these are survival, security, belonging, and esteem. (See Figure 2.)

The *survival needs* are those basic biological requirements necessary for life. When they are in short supply, discomfort is so great that almost all a student's energy can be commandeered until relief is found. Although extreme levels of physical deprivation may seldom appear in your classroom, students who are too hungry, too thirsty, too hot, too cold, or too uncomfortable will be hard to teach.

The *security needs* are students' strong tendencies to protect

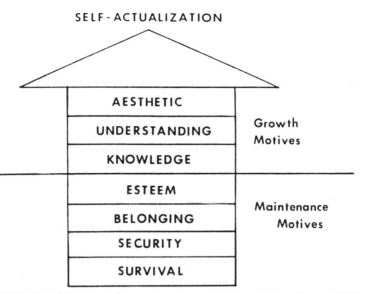

FIGURE 2 / Maslow's hierarchy of needs (adapted from Root, 1970).

themselves against hurt and discomfort. Fear and anxiety are unusually potent motivators. Various pressure groups have learned that people will do almost anything to avoid severe pain or death. One recent study (Gnagey, 1980) found that disruptive high school students had significantly stronger security needs than those who were cooperative in the classroom.

Next in descending order of potency are the *needs for belonging.* Students strive to be accepted and valued by their teachers and classmates. They will often act against their own values and the wishes of their parents in order to be accepted by their peers. The social isolates or rejects in your classes often become disciplinary problems as well.

When your students, survival, security, and belonging needs are satisfied, *esteem needs* come into play. Much of their energy is then directed into activities that make them feel like worthy, competent people. These feelings are a part of what psychologists call *self-concept.* Students who make trouble in school often lack self-esteem and have a very low self-concept.

Maslow insists that one's maintenance needs must be fairly well satiated before several *growth needs* can motivate human behavior.

These higher needs differ from the maintenance needs because the more they are fulfilled, the stronger they get. Maslow lists knowledge, aesthetic, and self-actualization needs in this higher category.

The *need to know and understand* one's world is often listed as an intrinsic need. Students who are "turned on" by discovering new knowledge don't require external payoffs to keep them learning. The process seems to be self-perpetuating. Elaborate systems of discovery learning and problem solving are based on this need to explore.

Aesthetic needs are people's desires for order and beauty. Whenever they discover or create beautiful things, they seem stimulated to pursue their aesthetic activities even further. Art exhibits, concerts, displays, house redecorating, all these are aimed at satisfying the aesthetic needs.

At the pinnacle of Maslow's hierarchy of human motives is *self-actualization*. When the lower needs have been sufficiently fulfilled, people strive to become in actuality what they are potentially. Hobbies often serve this purpose when people pursue them just because they see the hobbies as fulfilling activities.

So each student's hierarchy of needs is central to his/her motivational potential. The effective teacher provides a classroom environment that satisfies as many of these needs as possible. This not only prevents frustration-based misbehavior, but it also allows the student to respond to needs that are higher on the list. Need-fulfilling learning activities will help students direct their energies into educational pursuits instead of into annoying and wasteful disruptions.

Arousal Is Essential

Arousal refers to the level of a student's attention. If your learning activities keep students' arousal levels about midway between the extremes of slumber and panic, they will perform with optimal effectiveness. If you can focus attention on the skills and knowledge to be learned, discipline problems will virtually disappear. Teachers who wish to arouse and direct student attention must learn to manipulate relevance, complexity, intensity, novelty, and incongruity.

Relevant stimuli are those associated with need fulfillment.

Students who are experiencing strong needs for belonging will be presensitized to any signals of acceptance from their teachers and classmates. The more opportunities a teacher provides for appropriate need fulfillment, the more of the students' attention is grasped.

Complex stimuli hold attention longer than simple, obvious ones. It is as though the more complex ones present a challenge to "figure out," whereas the simple ones are fathomed at a glance. The effective teacher presents pictures, diagrams, explanations, and ideas that are just complex enough to be a challenge to most of the students.

Broadcasters have long used an increase in *intensity* of stimuli to grab the attention of their audience. The loud, color-filled TV ads continue to awaken listeners rudely in order to pander the wares of the sponsors. Experienced teachers know how to raise their voices just enough to focus attention, but not enough to startle their charges into overstimulation.

Creative teachers whose unique use of the language and inventive approach to instruction enthralls their students make excellent use of *novelty*. Misbehavior that results from boredom doesn't often materialize in such classrooms. Excellent teachers have found a constructive balance between the security of routines and the excitement of novel approaches to learning.

One of the most arousing situations in the classroom involves *incongruity*. Whenever a teacher can bring about a perceptual conflict, attention is high. Describing some "impossible" situation, showing a "mysterious trick, or presenting other discrepant events all capture student attention almost immediately. Teachers who can use such incongruous focal points as springboards into academic discovery seldom have to deal with counterproductive inattention.

Teachers who can use these principles to arouse their students' attention and keep it focused on learning activities have mastered another important facet of good discipline.

Expectancy Influences Effort

Another basic component of motivation is *expectancy*, one's anticipation of the rewards or punishments that may be consequences of a given activity. Energy is channeled into responses that promise need fulfullment and pleasure. It is seldom expended in pursuits that threaten frustration and discomfort. Data that are used to make such predictions result from past experience, vicarious experience, persuasion, and information.

Students' *past experiences* have taught them what to expect of the future. Students who have succeeded in your subject before will have confidence that they will pass your course. Others with a history of failure will approach your class with strong misgivings. This latter group is more often responsible for disruptive behaviors that call for disciplinary action.

Vicarious experience also influences student expectancy. Whenever past experience seems an inadequate basis for prediction, students look to see what happens to others in the contemplated situation. When disruptors are dealt with immediately, firmly, and consistently, their classmates predict a similar fate for themselves. If students garner obvious rewards for following the class rules, others in the audience expect similar consequences to follow their own conforming behaviors.

When data from past and vicarious experiences are not overpowering, students often base their predictions on the *opinions* of people they admire and respect. Such *persuasive* teachers and peers may exert considerable influence on what others in the class expect to happen. This makes it particularly important for teachers to gain the respect and cooperation of *student leaders*.

When there is little or no data available from other sources, a student's expectations may be influenced by new *information*. Teachers who provide accurate facts at the appropriate time can contribute a constructive influence on student expectancy.

Teachers can manipulate these four components of expectancy in such a way that students become more accurate and realistic about setting their goals. When this is accomplished, frustration is substantially reduced and students are not afraid to try new things because of unfounded fears of failure.

Rewards Perpetuate Responses

Whenever a student's actions are followed by need fulfillment or other pleasant feelings and sensations, we say those responses have been *rewarded.* Since such successful behaviors tend to be repeated, psychologists say they have been *reinforced.*

The effective teacher engineers learning activities so that rewards follow any movement toward the class goals and are never available following behavior that is counterproductive. While this seems obvious and "common sense," it does not happen without a great deal of organized planning and vigilance. The vast amount of literature written about behavior modification attests to this.

Punishment Suppresses Some Responses

The actual negative consequences that follow some action are called *punishment.* Since such experiences threaten our extremely potent security needs, we tend to avoid them at all costs. One type of punishment consists of *aversive stimuli* such as pain and other unpleasant feelings and sensations. Both physical and verbal spankings are examples of this category. But the *removal of expected rewards* also functions as punishment. Any system of fines is an example of this type too, even though the reinforcers are removed after they have been applied.

Good disciplinarians arrange their activities so that punishments never follow a student's movements toward class goals, but only follow counterproductive responses. Although students usually do not repeat behaviors that are punished, the fear and resentment that accompanies the administration of penalties may spawn new acts of anger and revenge for the teacher to deal with.

SUMMARY AND DISCUSSION

An analog model is presented to illustrate the interaction of five categories of influence on student motivation—the tendency to expend energy doing one thing rather than another. This model consists of five interrelated forces: needs, arousal, expectancy, reward, and punishment. Teachers who help students fulfill maintenance needs like security, belonging, and esteem will not only have fewer disciplinary problems, but will enable their pupils to respond to higher growth needs like knowledge, aesthetics, and self-actualization.

Teachers can draw their students' attention away from distracting stimuli by introducing relevant, complex, intense, novel, and sometimes incongruous stimuli into their lessons. When students expect to learn and succeed in school, they tend to facilitate class activities, but fear of failure can be a cause for disruptive behavior.

When the teacher engineers his or her class so that appropriate rewards follow productive behavior, students learn and are well behaved. Punishments should be minimized and used only after counterproductive behaviors.

The good disciplinarian uses these principles of motivation to cause students to expend their energy on learning instead of wasting it on misbehaving. In the succeeding chapters of this book we shall describe concrete methods for improving classroom discipline. As you shall see, nearly every one can be related to our model of motivation.

FEEDBACK QUIZ

1. Motivation is composed of all the forces that cause a person to (a) accept the teacher's goals, (b) behave well in class, (c) expend energy doing something, (d) learn school material.
2. Aversive feelings that result from biological and psychological disequilibria are called (a) goals, (b) needs, (c) pain, (d) values.
3. According to Maslow, which of the following maintenance needs must be satiated first? (a) belonging, (b) esteem, (c) security, (d) survival.
4. When people do things that they think will make them better people, they are responding to _____ needs. (a) belonging, (b) esteem, (c) security, (d) survival.
5. According to Maslow, which of the following growth needs is at the top of the hierarchy? (a) aesthetic, (b) knowledge, (c) self-actualization.
6. Compared to the growth needs, the maintenance needs (a) are

higher on the hierarchy, (b) get stronger when they are fulfilled, (c) are less basic to survival, (d) must be satiated first.

7. Students will learn most effectively when their arousal level is (a) high, (b) low, (c) moderate.

8. Which of the following characteristics of arousal-producing experiences involves fulfilling student needs? (a) complexity, (b) incongruity, (c) intensity, (d) relevance.

9. Brightly colored visual aids create arousal because of their (a) complexity, (b) incongruity, (c) intensity, (d) relevance.

10. When a person is motivated by the rewards or punishments that he or she expects, _____ is at work. (a) arousal, (b) expectancy, (c) need deprivation, (d) persuasion.

11. When one student expects to be rewarded for an act because he or she has seen someone else rewarded for it, _____ is at work. (a) information, (b) past experience, (c) persuasion, (d) vicarious experience.

12. Students tend to _____ behavior that has been rewarded. (a) avoid, (b) forget, (c) repeat, (d) suppress.

13. Behaviors that are followed by punishment are usually (a) avoided, (b) forgotten, (c) repeated, (d) repressed.

14. When anticipated rewards are _____, this action functions as punishment. (d) doubled, (b) ignored, (c) reinforced, (d) withheld.

15. Even if punishment reduces the misbehaviors that precede it, it may also increase a student's (a) anger, (b) appreciation, (c) confidence, (d) intelligence.

Three

Problem Teachers: Avoiding Ineffective Leadership

1. Describe the *despot* and list several negative side effects of this kind of leadership.

2. Explain how the *flirt* caused increased classroom misbehavior and why young teachers must be especially careful to avoid this style.

3. List and explain several reasons for the chaos that may result if a teacher attempts to be a *nonentity*.

4. Using the motivational model in Chapter 2, explain how the despot, the flirt, and the *nonentity* misused its five components.

Carol Denler burst into tears. She was sure that she could never become a good accounting teacher and she was ready to quit school.

Mr. Joel, her college supervisor, was quite unprepared for this sudden and unexpected disaster. In his most professional manner, he tried to quiet the young student teacher so that they could make some sense of the situation. Several Kleenex tissues later, the following story emerged:

Ms. Denler had been assigned to Mr. Thomas's business classes for twelve weeks of student teaching. Mr. Thomas, an expert critic teacher, had begun in the usual way by allowing Carol to observe his methods and get used to the class situation. Gradually he had worked her into the schedule until she was handling a full load of typing, shorthand, and accounting classes. Everything seemed to be going well when the one accounting class suddenly became unmanageable.

The girls in this class unaccountably turned on Ms. Denler and seemed bent on sabotaging her every plan. They refused to hand in their papers on time. They made barely audible remarks about her appearance when she was trying to explain the work to the class. There were even several instances of out-and-out defiance of the rules she was trying to enforce.

Because she was afraid that Mr. Thomas would give her a low

grade in student teaching, she had kept these incidents a secret until the situation got so bad that she had fled to her college supervisor in despair.

Fifteen minutes after Ms. Denler left, Mr. Joel was talking to the critic teacher on the phone. Mr. Thomas apologized for not looking in more often and promised to get to the bottom of the situation the next morning. He added that his student secretary was a member of the class and could help him fill in the details with more accuracy. At four the next afternoon, the critic teacher made the following revealing report to the college supervisor.

The boys in the accounting class had become quite infatuated with their teacher. They found out by trial and error that every time they asked for help with a posting problem, she would seat herself on the table near them, lean down close to them, and make suggestions about how the problem should be approached. Reinforced by her proximity, the boys deluged her with posting questions and vied with one another for her attentions.

According to Mr. Thomas's frank secretary, Ms. Denler was taking an unfair advantage of her position as a student teacher and had no business flirting with "their boys." The secretary added that Ms. Denler wore her skirts too short and her blouses too tight for a teacher. She admitted openly that the girls hated the student teacher and were out to cut her academic throat.

When Mr. Joel explained the situation to Ms. Denler, she was aghast. It was obvious from the look of disbelief on her face that she had been completely oblivious to what had been going on in the accounting class. She was so embarrassed that Mr. Joel was afraid she wouldn't go back to the class the next day.

Showing more pluck than he had expected, Ms. Denler did return to her duties in the accounting class. For the rest of the time, she observed three rules carefully: she dressed in apparel that could not possibly be construed as provocative, answered the boys' questions in a businesslike manner from a discrete distance, and never sat on the tables again. She received an A in student teaching for that term.

Ms. Denler's dilemma is a dramatic but not uncommon example of the fact that there are many situations in which teachers may unwittingly cause students in their class to become deviant. In this chapter we will explore several of these situations so that our readers may understand and avoid them.

WHAT LEADERSHIP STYLES CAUSE STUDENT MISBEHAVIOR?

In later chapters we shall specify specific teacher behaviors that prevent or promote student misbehaviors. In this section we describe several general approaches to teaching that appear to incite disciplinary problems rather than solve them.

The Despot

Despots embrace a *custodial* view of pupil control. Their primary concern is maintaining order. They tend to stereotype students in terms of their appearance, behavior, and parents' socioeconomic status. Despots perceive students as irresponsible, undisciplined people who must be controlled through punishment. These teachers view misbehavior in moralistic terms and take each violation as a personal affront. They maintain impersonal relationships with their students and expect them to accept the despot's decisions without question (Willower, Eidell, and Hoy, 1973). Goldstein and Weber (1979) have recently demonstrated a negative relationship between this authoritarian approach and "on task behavior" in the classroom.

The despot has been called a tyrant, sadist, hard-boiled autocrat, and many other less complimentary names, but his or her intent seems always the same—to call all the shots. In one of those delightful flights of fantasy that caricature a person by carrying his behaviors to the absurd, one academic despot's orders were reenacted in the following ways by one of his fifth-grade subjects. "Now you may open your books. Now you may read. Now you may put your name in the upper left-hand corner two centimeters from the edge. Now you may practice your spelling list. Now you may go to the lavatory. Now you may breathe!"

In a way the despot establishes a sort of permanent atmosphere of frustration in the classroom, rewarding only the willing serfs for their efforts.

You will not be surprised to learn that most students respond to the despot with a great deal of anger, but you may be unaware of some of the ways this anger is displayed.

If the tyrant is formidable enough, the anger may never be turned against him, at least not in his presence. Several studies have shown that students often wait until the leader is absent before they give vent to their aggression. Ms. Stroud was a sturdy woman who ruled the fifth grade with an iron hand. Things always went well in her little kingdom and behavior problems were virtually unthinkable. Any unfortunate deviant who forgot his or her place for a moment was soon terrified into submission. The glowering advance of this hulking woman was enough to make the bravest Jack in the class slide hurriedly back down his beanstalk to safety.

But one morning the building custodian was witness to an awesome sight. Vandals had broken into the school sometime over the weekend and had virtually laid waste to Ms. Stroud's room. Files were overturned, money was stolen, and ink was splashed on the walls and desks. Every window had been shattered from the inside, and papers were scattered about in complete disarray. One could almost visualize the anger that had been unleashed in that room the night before.

The janitor, hurrying into the adjacent social studies room, hardly dared predict what damage he might find there. To his surprise, neat piles of ballots were still in place awaiting the mock election to be held in class the next day. A sum of money collected for the Heart Fund was still safe in the unlocked top desk drawer. Nothing in that room had been touched by the weekend intruders.

As in all too many cases of this kind, the vandals were never caught, but those who understand the feelings that are stirred up by the dictator wouldn't be surprised to learn that Ms. Stroud had been partly responsible for this destructive insurrection.

But formidable tyrants like Ms. Stroud often cause other more serious deviancies of which they may not even be aware. In order to protect themselves, students serving under a teacher-dictator form their own "gestapo." As mass punishment is often used when the teacher is unable to find a culprit, the children protect themselves by informing on each other. A regular secret service develops, to the point where a would-be deviant is convinced that even the walls have ears.

If the dictator becomes ill, an explosive situation may await an unsuspecting substitute teacher. If he or she tries to use more democratic methods or is a bit less formidable as an autocrat, the students may literally run the teacher out. Unfortunately, assistant principals often interpret this as a sign of incompetence on the part of the substitute and put him or her on their blacklist. Sadder still, the same administrators may laud the dictator as an exemplary teacher because that person "can handle tough classes."

Finally, the anger generated in the students of such an autocrat may be displaced on one or more of the class weaklings after school. Frank Buck is supposed to have revealed the fact that he was never able to bring the weakest monkeys back alive.[1] After several healthy monkeys were captured and put in a cage for shipment, the weakest one or two were invariably dead on arrival at their destination.

Many a parent is at a loss to understand why the other children taunt or beat up one child night after night on the way home from school. When situations like this are investigated, it often develops that the child is one who can't or won't fight back. The frustration-triggered angers of the day can be safely displaced on those who will absorb the punishment. In those cases where a child seems to ask for trouble, a day with a tyrant will almost assure him of getting it.

Occasionally, some teacher tries to play the role of the dictator and fails. When the frustrations are great and the threat of punishment lacks conviction, a "fifth column" soon develops to sabotage the teacher. Unlike the case of the successful dictator, the students cohere against the teacher and victimize only those who like him or her (Redl, 1942).

Ms. Toll was hired to teach English in a rural high school at the edge of a small village. Believing that a successful teacher must "start tough," she assumed the role of a dictator for the greater part of the first semester. Afraid that she would be unsuccessful, she was unnecessarily sarcastic and made petty and unrealistic demands on her students. Several times boys in the class were moved to open defiance of her authority and found that she did not carry out her threats. Planned deviancies began to increase. Books were dropped on the floor at prearranged signals, chalk and erasers disappeared just before the teacher was going to use them, and weird noises constantly emanated from different locations in the room when the teacher's back was turned.

One day about the middle of the year the class saboteurs had drawn up a master deviancy plan. They obtained a supply of ex-

[1] Frank Howard Buck (1884–1950) was an American jungle explorer who secured wild life without hurting them and sold them to U.S. zoos. He wrote *Bring 'Em Back Alive* in 1930.

ploding toy caps and placed two in the steel supports of each desk seat in the English room. When the first-hour class came in and flopped resignedly in their seats, the sharp staccato of thirty-five cap explosions bombarded the air. Taken completely unaware, Ms. Toll fled the room in tears, amid the nervous laughter of her class. She was unable to return to her post that semester and had to be replaced by substitutes for the remainder of the year.

The malevolent despot may be a direct or indirect cause of many deviancies. If they do not occur in his or her presence, they may take place while the despot is gone; or they may be displaced on innocent third parties at other times. When entire schools can be characterized as custodial, students exhibit a great sense of power-lessness and normlessness (Rafalides and Hoy, 1971). They show low self-actualization and feel more at the mercy of outside forces (Deibert and Hoy, 1977).

The Flirt

Ms. Denler, whose story opened this chapter, was an example of an unwitting flirt. Redl (1942) would describe her as the "object of affectional drives." Other less psychoanalytic observers might just say that the boys had a crush on her. This phenomenon occurs most often at the high-school level, as this is the time that adolescents are making the transition from their parents as love objects to others nearer their own age. An intermediate stage in the process is often a more mature individual, like a teacher, who possesses both parental and peer-love-object qualities. The fresh-out-of-college teacher fits this category all too well.

In Ms. Denler's case, deviancies arose because of the feelings engendered in the students of her own sex. They felt that their chances of making a hit with the boys were thwarted by Ms. Denler's presence and actions and proceeded to direct their aggression at the person whom they perceived to be the cause of the frustrating situation. The fact that the student teacher allowed herself to be flattered by the boys' attention made matters inestimably worse. It was only after she ceased her familiarity with the boys that she regained control of the class. Boys can become similarly irritated with a male teacher who flirts with the girls in their class.

Although not related closely to classroom deviancy as such, there are other knotty problems that can arise for the teacher who is unaware of his or her position as a flirt. Jim Friend always made his colleagues at Middleton High feel as though he cared a great deal about each of them. When Jim met them in the hall, he never rushed by with the usual "Hello" or "How are you" that one expects. Invariably he would stop, put his hand on his fellow teacher's shoulder, and talk briefly about something of mutual interest.

For this reason, teachers at Middleton were shocked to hear that Jim was being called before the school board on a morals charge. An inquiry into the situation brought to light the following story. One of the high-school girls developed a crush on Mr. Friend and began to stop him in the hall and on the street on one pretext or another. As was his custom, Jim Friend often talked to his female student with his hand on her shoulder. This habit, together with an active imagination on the part of the student, soon had started the story that Mr. Friend was taking indecent liberties with the girls at the high school. Several parents called the principal to protest the rehiring of such a teacher. One member of the school board demanded a special meeting to face Mr. Friend with the charges. Although Jim Friend was finally exonerated of all charges, it was a most uncomfortable year for him at Middleton High.

In order to illustrate that the flirt is probably always at least in part responsible for his or her own troubles, let it be said that those teachers who fail to respond to amorous signals and who consistently show no favorites soon discourage this brand of idolatry. There are some teachers, on the other hand, whose own needs prompt them to respond in ways that make the matter much worse.

Jill Star was hired to teach at Mill Center. Her collegiate record was quite excellent, and the principal felt fortunate to have obtained her to replace a teacher who was retiring. When the boys from senior English saw the new teacher walk into the room, several were moved to make low whistles of admiration and were overjoyed when she blushed obviously and became visibly flustered. Though she quickly regained her poise, it was apparent to all that the attention had gotten to her.

In the months that followed, the boys tried many strategies to gain her favor. For some unknown reason, Ms. Star chose to discipline all deviants by making them sit in front of the class near her desk. Several boys took the bait and vied with each other for this position of honor, where they would gaze fondly at her. This action brought more blushes from Jill, and less English was taught with each succeeding day. Although a friendly principal tried to point out ways that disciplinary trouble could be avoided, the young teacher could not seem to extricate herself from the situation.

On the night of graduation, Ms. Star went out on a date with a senior boy, confirming the principal's suspicion that there was more to the bad situation than a few obstreperous students. As the board was outspoken on such matters, she was asked to resign immediately.

Although the flirt may not wish it so, he or she has become a love object for one or more students. In- and out-of-school deviancies may result, if the teacher does not take steps to prove that she or he is a mature adult who is interested in students as such and is not vulnerable to their attempts to start a romantic relationship.

The Nonentity

Mr. Gale was convinced that one of the greatest ills of public school education was its suppression of the creative impulses of its students. Having read and applauded articles about "other-directed persons who become sheep in gray flannel suits," he was determined that in his art class no such crime would be perpetrated. His approach was to lay out the materials necessary for work with several media and retreat to his own canvas, allowing each student to initiate an individual project and carry it out at his own speed. Mr. Gale made it quite clear to his students that their grade would not depend upon how many projects they turned out.

When a student came to him for help, he would reflect the inquiry in his best Rogerian manner and refuse to give any prescriptions. If pressed for more direction, Benjamin Gale would invariably describe three or four approaches and leave it to the student to decide which to use.

After a few weeks of this treatment, several different phenomena began to take shape. A revolving card game developed in the far corner among the boys who had taken art for a snap course. Little knots of giggling girls would assemble daily by the windows overlooking the athletic field. Several students brought textbooks from other subjects and used the period to catch up. Little scuffling bits of horseplay were on the increase, and the number of students who worked seriously at a project became fewer and fewer.

The climax to the story came on a Friday when three events brought Mr. Gale out of retirement. Dick Snead was one of the few students whom Mr. Gale considered to have real artistic promise. From the first day Dick had seemed eager to begin work and kept at it until he had arrived late several times at his next class. In his own mind Mr. Gale thought of Dick as a sort of human proof that his technique of teaching was effective. The week before, Mr. Gale had had to exert considerable self-control to keep from pointing out a perspective error that he knew would eventually ruin the effect of Dick's painting. But sounds of muffled fury emanated from behind Dick's canvas, and Mr. Gale was horrified to see the muscular lad slash his hard work to ribbons and stamp unceremoniously out the door.

Visibly agitated by Dick's violent exit, the others began milling about nervously. Even the card game broke up. Two boys were soon pushing each other in prelude to a fight. Bits of clay began to fly about the room, spattering here and there on the white walls. The volcano was preparing to erupt.

At this instant Mr. Volker, the principal, stepped into the room. Somehow avoiding the barrage of clay, he shouted the mob down, banished them all to study hall for the rest of the hour, and ordered them to show up after school to clean up the mess. For the next thirty minutes Mr. Gale and Mr. Volker planned some drastic reforms in the way art would be taught in the days to come.

Glickman and Wolfgang would classify Mr. Gale as a *non-interventionist*. They note that, "The non-interventionists believe in a supportive, facilitating environment where the teacher is present to accept and empathize with the child in his or her inner struggle" (1979, p. 7). A number of studies have described the counter-productive effects of an impersonal, laissez-faire approach to leadership (Thompson, 1944; White, 1953; Ryans, 1952; Goldstein and Weber, 1979). The teacher who is overpermissive, even for idealistic reasons, may be in for trouble. Without any structure, even art becomes filled with unpleasant feelings of pointlessness. For the earnest novice who sets his or her goals too high, a teacher who refuses to lend an expert hand in times of frustration may be a party to both deviancy and disillusionment.

SUMMARY AND DISCUSSION

Several counterproductive leadership styles have been described in this chapter. Each of them has misused some elements of motivation, thereby causing student misbehavior.

The malevolent despot managed to frustrate rather than to fulfill almost all student needs. Because punishment was so regularly and indiscriminately administered, students looked forward to class with fear, anxiety, and resentment. The only rewards that were forthcoming consisted of avoiding pain and discomfort. This pathological situation not only caused students to use all their energies trying to fulfill their maintenance needs, but succeeded in making them so angry that they became overaggressive and destructive.

The flirt frustrated the belonging needs of half the class and led the other half to expect her to be a love object for them. Rewards were given for amorous behavior instead of for learning, so that the boys' goals ceased to be focused on the academic tasks at hand. This competitive situation frustrated the girls to the point where their anger was vented on the flirt herself.

The nonentity refused to make any motivational moves at all. Since inexperienced students were allowed to set goals for themselves, many expected success that was not possible at their skill level. This frustrated self-esteem needs and made the experience an unpleasant one. Since the teacher remained aloof and left students on their own, he failed to provide rewards for work well done and for appropriate behavior. Neither did he make any attempt to arouse his students or to focus their attention on their work. As a result, they were easily distracted by almost any other stimuli. Evidently he was also incapable of administering effective punishment, since the principal was forced to step in and take over the class.

Now that we have exposed some leadership styles that are counterproductive in the classroom, we will move on to a discussion of some student characteristics that predispose classroom disorder.

1. Which of the following counterproductive teaching styles may motivate vandalism? (a) despot, (b) flirt, (c) nonentity.

2. Under which teacher style do students often attempt things that are much too difficult for them? (a) despot, (b) flirt, (c) nonentity.

3. Which of the teacher styles exemplifies the *custodial* view of pupil control by Willower and others? (a) despot, (b) flirt, (c) nonentity.

4. Which of the teacher styles is called a *noninterventionist* by Glickman and Wolfgang? (a) despot, (b) flirt, (c) nonentity.

5. A formidable despot usually causes students' anger to be (a) considerably reduced, (b) displaced on others, (c) turned inward, (d) vented on the teacher.

6. Which of the teacher styles involves a great deal of jealousy? (a) despot, (b) flirt, (c) nonentity.

7. Which of the five components of motivation was the only one *not* misused by the despot? (a) arousal, (b) expectancy, (c) needs, (d) punishment, (e) reward.

8. Which of the girls' maintenance needs was frustrated by the flirt? (a) belonging, (b) esteem, (c) security, (d) survival.

9. Which maintenance need was frustrated when the nonentity's students attempted projects beyond their ability? (a) belonging, (b) esteem, (c) security, (d) survival.

10. The nonentity failed to make use of any of the components of motivation, but his ineffectiveness in _____ caused his students to be easily distracted. (a) arousal, (b) expectancy, (c) needs, (d) punishment, (e) reward.

Four

The Disruptive Student: Why Can't Johnny/ Jenny Behave?

1. Explain why ignorance of classroom rules may cause students to misbehave.

2. Give three illustrations of behaviors learned in non-middle-class homes that conflict with middle-class school rules.

3. Explain how television may cause some students to get in trouble at school.

4. Explain what is meant by the frustration-aggression hypothesis.

5. List and describe three agents of frustration that operate in the classroom.

6. Explain what is meant when we say the negative relationship between achievement and misbehavior is probably circular.

7. Explain how an external locus of control can increase academic frustration.

8. List three situations that may cause a student to displace negative emotions in the classroom.

9. Explain how anxiety-produced misbehavior differs from disruptions caused by frustration.

10. Relate our motivational model to your answers to 1, 2, 5, 8, and 9 above.

Larruping Larry—a small blond tiger with flailing fists—was at it again. Battle One had occurred on the way to school that morning, and the safeties had not considered it serious enough to report to the principal. Battle Two had taken place in gym class during the second school hour and got Larry an F in deportment for the day. Now here he was again in the "drink of water and lavatory line" pummeling the boy in front of him as though his life depended on it.

Mr. Grange hauled him out of line and held him firmly until the flailing ceased. He was glad to be dealing with the soft little fists of a six-year-old and tried to imagine, momentarily, what he would do if Larry were fifteen. Dismissing the thought with the rueful recognition that he was woefully out of shape, Jack Grange led the subdued Larry back to the science room and began to go through the ancient, stereotyped ritual of scolding, threatening, and punishing that seems to rise up unbidden from the deep wells of a teacher's subconscious.

But Jack's mind withdrew for a moment, allowing the rest of his organism to continue the time-honored routine. "What's gotten into this formidable little tyke?" he mused. "What makes him so hard to handle? What sets him off like that? What kind of an approach might really get to the core of the trouble?"

As Mr. Grange's mind and body fused once more, he found himself sending Larry off to homeroom with the final "no more fights today" cliché! As the explosive little chap trudged off down the

hall, Mr. Jack Grange, elementary science teacher, knew that he had
failed the child once again. But there was the sixth grade, already
restless in their seats, waiting to be enlightened about the probable
atmospheric conditions of Saturn and Jupiter.

WHAT MAKES STUDENTS MISBEHAVE?

Mr. Grange's question about what had "gotten into" Larry is a
carry-over from ancient times, when the demon theory was accepted.
At that time the answer to all such questions lay in the type of evil
spirit that had entered the child's body. Another current phrase, "I
don't know what possessed him," arises from the same mystical approach. About the only thing to recommend such a theory is its im-
plication that something outside the deviant is influencing his actions. There is no doubt that his self-control is limited by his past
experience.

Ignorance

Ignorance of the rules is certainly one of the reasons for a child be-
coming a deviant. This is especially true during his first encounter
with a teacher. Even if a student is presented with a neatly organized set of bylaws, he never really knows which statutes are operational and which are just on paper. As every seasoned substitute
teacher knows, classes have a very practical way of solving this
problem. They simply proceed to try the teacher out, to see what
they can get away with.

Lest you think that the trying-out procedure is a proof of the in-
nate perversity of students, it should be pointed out that being in a
situation where they really don't know the ground rules can be very
anxiety-producing. It is analogous to diving into a gravel-pit swimming hole without being sure where the sharp rocks and bales of
barbed wire are situated. Kounin, Gump, and Ryan (1961) found

that even kindergarten children were able to differentiate between the verbal and actual rules of the classroom at the end of their first week in school.

Conflicting Rules

Conflicting social rulebooks is another reason why students become deviants. William C. Kvareceus (1945) pointed out long ago that many delinquents have learned the lessons of their neighborhoods too well. When the behaviors that brought results at home are deemed improper or immoral at school, a student becomes the victim of negative transfer of training. Teachers born and trained in a middle-class "cloister" are apt to be traumatized by the language and appearance of children who come from the center-of-the-city homes. Many a show-and-tell period has been discontinued because the teacher could not bear either the subjects that were talked about or the language used in telling. McGinnis and Smitherman (1978) argue that a great deal of conflict may center around a school system's attempt to force black children to reduce their use of the black English they have learned in their homes.

The lad who has learned that the way to gain status in his neighborhood is to knock down every kid that taunts him is in for a great surprise when he tries to operate this way in most public schools. Over 20 years ago Kagan (1958) pointed out that many child behaviors were just imitations of some adult model. If that model behaves in ways that are not acceptable to the teacher in a given situation, the hapless mimic is in for trouble indeed. A minority student may even have learned an unacceptable response to punishment. Brophy and Putnam (1979, p. 184) point to evidence that while middle-class teachers expect students to "look them straight in the eye" while they are being reprimanded, their parents would interpret such behavior as a sign of open defiance. Liefer, Gordon, and Graves (1974) have shown that even violent models on TV can influence a student's aggressive behavior.

It is obvious that a number of students may become deviants merely because they have failed to discriminate between the rules of the home and school situations.

Reactions to thwarting often take the form of deviancies in the classroom. Since John Dollard (1939) and others posed their frustration-aggression hypothesis, the connection between need deprivation and angry behavior has been well documented.

There are at least three agents of frustration in a classroom that may impinge upon any student: the teacher, the classmates, and the activities. Any and all of these could push a student toward deviancy.

There were, no doubt, a number of students in Mr. Linkers' algebra class (Chapter 1) who were frustrated by the dentention period thrust upon them by Mr. Beggs, the principal. It would not have been surprising to see the number of deviants increase after such mass punishment. As the person in charge of the classroom, a teacher is often thrust into the role of chief frustrator. In Chapter 3, the despot is characterized as an extreme example of this role.

A second source of thwarting may be the deviant's classmates. Lee Cronbach (1977, p. 189) asserts that peer approval is a strong and basic need, often motivating student behavior. If a student is an isolate or reject in his own classroom, he might be expected to react with aggression to this intolerable situation.

Lorber (1966) found that children who are socially unacceptable to their classmates tend to act in a disruptive, attention-seeking manner in the classroom. Conger (1973) concluded that delinquents have poor peer relationships all the way from elementary school through high school. Johnson and Johnson (1974) point out that competitive goal structures can increase interstudent friction and destroy an effective classroom climate.

Since academic achievement is the major goal of schooling, inability to learn is a major source of student frustration. The relationship between achievement problems and misbehavior is well established. Both Conger (1973) and Duke (1976) concluded that students with chronic behavior problems performed poorly in school and on tests of basic skills. The relationship is probably circular.

In a comparison of achievement test scores of high school inhibitors (disruptive students) and facilitators (well-behaved students), Gnagey (1979) found that the mean percentile rank of inhibitors was about half that of their facilitator counterparts. An earlier study

(Jorgenson, 1977) concluded that the easier school material became for students, the more their classroom behavior improved.

Eaves (1978) found a significant relationship between reading disability and hostility, even in students of above-average intelligence.

Another influence on frustration-produced misbehavior may reside in the way students have learned to explain their own successes and failures. In a second study of high school inhibitors and facilitators, Gnagey (1980) found that disruptive students had a significantly more external locus of control than well-behaved students. Their belief that their successes and failures are caused by forces outside themselves is the sort of learned helplessness that makes academic frustration even stronger.

Displacement

Displaced feelings account for the misbehavior of some deviants. Just as inappropriate actions may be transferred into the classroom from the outside environment, so inappropriate feelings are often displaced on the people and objects in the school. Bernadine was quite open about the fact that she could not stand Mr. Williams or his social studies class. She was always mumbling something nasty under her breath or bursting into tears at the slightest hint of disciplinary action. She assiduously avoided him in the hallway and refused to cooperate with him in any way.

Upon talking with the other teachers who taught Bernadine, Mr. Williams was aghast to find that his troublesome student seemed to be a model young lady in all the rooms except his. He took his problem to the assistant principal, where the following story was revealed.

Bernadine and her mother lived in a cold-water flat together. The father had just left them for the third time that year. Frequently over the past six months, the father had come home drunk and beaten his wife and daughter savagely. Both mother and daughter were convinced that men were beasts. Poor Mr. Williams was the only male teacher in the building and was the unwilling recipient of Bernadine's father-inspired hatred.

In a study by Thruston, Feldhusen, and Benning (1973), several of the following factors appeared again and again in the home situations of children who were constant classroom deviants:

1. The discipline by the father is either lax, overly strict, or erratic.
2. The supervision by the mother is at best only fair, or it is downright inadequate.
3. The parents are either indifferent or even hostile toward the child.
4. The family members are scattered in diverse activities and operate only somewhat as a unit or perhaps not at all.
5. The parents find it difficult to talk things over regarding the child.
6. The husband-wife relationship lacks closeness and equality or partnership.
7. The parents find many things to disapprove of in their child.
8. The mothers are not happy with the communitities in which they live.
9. The parents resort to angry physical punishment when the child does wrong. Temper control is a difficult problem for them at this time.
10. The parents believe they have little influence on the development of their child.
11. The parents believe that other children exert bad influences on their child.
12. The parents' leisuretime activities lack much of a constructive element.
13. The parents, particularly the father, report no church membership. Even if they are members, their attendance tends to be sporadic.

Lefkowitz and his colleagues (1973) found significant correlations between parental rejection and aggressive school behavior.

The transfer into the classroom of the parent-inspired hostilities of such children could certainly be at the base of their perennial deviancy. Hillman (1972) has found a significant relationship between a child's family makeup and his or her school behavior. Searcy-Miller and her associates (1977) have shown that even the size of a student's family influences the type of maladjustment that shows up in the school setting.

Sam was always taking mean digs at the other students in Ms.

Smedly's class. He not only made fun of their recitations and art work, but often poked them with his pencil or tripped them on the playground. In addition, Sam seemed to have an inordinate need for Ms. Smedly's approval. It seemed as though he was always shouldering aside the others to gain the undivided limelight.

A brief talk with his mother revealed that Sam was a middle child in the family. He could not hope to compete successfully with the older brother, who was both a brilliant student and a natural athlete. When he tried out the baby talk that seemed to work for his younger brother, his parents told him to grow up and stop acting like a two-year-old. It was apparent that Sam had transferred into the schoolroom his angry feelings toward his brothers and was taking them out on his undeserving classmates.

Often a student may be difficult to deal with because he has a bad aftertaste from his experiences with another teacher or class. He may transfer his negative feelings for a cruel, sarcastic teacher to another who is really quite kind and considerate. A student who has learned to hate social studies in another school may misbehave in the social studies class in the new school simply because he has transferred those old feelings to a new situation. The unfortunate result is that he often causes the new teacher to feel the same way about him that the former one did, and the cycle begins all over again.

Although it is true that positive feelings are also transferred from old situations to new ones, they seldom pose any problems for the teacher. He or she usually assumes that student's good behavior is a direct and deserved result of pedagogical expertise.

Anxiety

Leffingwell (1977) argues that a great deal of student misbehavior may be caused by anxious reactions to taking tests, speaking in front of others, or being judged for performance. This view is supported by Gnagey's (1980) finding that the safety needs of disruptive students were much stronger (they were more afraid) than their well-behaved schoolmates.

In a cross-national survey, Peck and Hughes (1979) have shown that a child's skill in coping with such anxieties is predictive of school success.

It is probable that a number of student misbehaviors are prompted by the need to defend their egos against anxiety.

SUMMARY AND DISCUSSION

In this chapter we have described some disruptive students and some forces that probably contributed to their misbehavior. It is quite easy to relate these factors to our motivational model of human behavior (Chapter 2).

Both ignorance of the rules and conflicting rulebooks contribute to defects in student expectancy. If youngsters aren't told which behaviors will result in rewards or punishments, trial and error takes over. When home experiences have built expectancies that are contradicted at school, inappropriate behavior inevitably results.

Social and academic frustration refer to situations in which belonging and esteem needs are not being fulfilled. The resulting aggression, clowning, or cheating can become serious problems.

Displaced feelings are also a function of expectancy. When previous experience has taught students to expect parents, siblings, and teachers to be aversive, they anticipate similar treatment from similar people.

Anxiety is the result of strong unfulfilled safety needs. When students expect to fail or to be judged ineffective by others, they often resort to defensive behaviors designed to protect their self-concepts from injury. Such moves are often counterproductive to effective learning.

Now that we have discussed some teacher- and student-related forces that contribute to classroom misbehavior, Chapter 5 explains how to set up a list of rules that may counteract many of these destructive influences.

FEEDBACK QUIZ

1. When classroom rules are not clear, students often misbehave in order to (a) drive the teacher away, (b) find out what the rules are, (c) punish their classmates, (d) show their perversity.

2. Classroom misbehavior results when students' home rules are _____ the school rules. (a) different from, (b) stronger than, (c) the same as, (d) weaker than.

3. Research shows that watching violence on television causes students to act _____ at school. (a) less aggressively, (b) less violently, (c) more passively, (d) more violently.

4. According to the frustration-aggression hypothesis, angry behavior often results from (a) being reinforced for violent behavior, (b) imitating violent models, (c) need deprivation, (d) seeing deviants go unpunished.

5. Which of the following agents is responsible for social frustration in the classroom? (a) classmates, (b) physical environment, (c) subject matter, (d) teacher.

6. Student misbehavior is probably (a) caused by poor achievement, (b) the cause of poor achievement, (c) both a and b, (d) neither a nor b.

7. A student's frustration is probably increased if he or she attributes failures to (a) lack of personal effort, (b) lesson difficulty, (c) luck, (d) both b and c.

8. When classroom misbehavior results from displacement, students express feelings that result from (a) academic frustration, (b) classmate cruelty, (c) outside circumstances, (d) teacher control techniques.

9. When a student misbehavior can properly be classified as *defensive*, it is usually caused by (a) anxiety, (b) displacement, (c) frustration, (d) ignorance.

10. Ignorance of rules, displacement, and conflicting rulebooks result from inadequate (a) arousal, (b) expectancy, (c) needs, (d) punishment.

11. All kinds of frustration refer to inadequate (a) arousal stimuli, (b) displacement phenomena, (c) need fulfillment, (d) punishment.

12. Anxiety results when the _____ need is unfullfilled. (a) aesthetic, (b) safety, (c) self-actualization, (d) survival.

Five

Making Effective Rules: Defining Misbehavior

1. Distinguish between *behavior* and *misbehavior*.

2. List some deviancies that have continued to appear in educators' lists over the years.

3. List and describe five different considerations that influence a teacher's definition of *misbehavior*. Explain how *pupil control ideology* may affect each.

4. List and explain five ways to improve classroom rules. Show how they are related to the motivational model.

A second-grader recently took it upon himself to educate me about some of the facts of school life. I had merely asked him how his gym class was going and was unprepared for the lecture that followed.

"Just great!" he said. "Ever since Miss Brinker came, I really like gym. When Miss Crane used to teach us, she yelled at us all the time. We couldn't have any fun. But Miss Brinker doesn't care if you have a little fun. She is a beautiful teacher!"

Although I would certainly be unwilling to base a serious evaluation on the Misses Brinker and Crane on the exuberant statements of one small lad, he does make one important point without really meaning to: *What is misbehavior to some teachers is certainly not to others.* This chapter attempts to define misbehavior and describe several bases for judging an act to be deviant.

WHAT IS MISBEHAVIOR?

Someone has pointed out that a weed is any plant that grows where it is not wanted. A hybrid corn plant is just as much a weed in a flowerbed as a morning glory is in a cornfield. The classification of a plant as a weed is much more dependent on the purposes of the gardener than on any characteristic of the plant itself.

Our definition of misbehavior draws a close parallel to the one above: *Misbehavior* is any action that is taken where it is not wanted. A quiet, businesslike demeanor at a party may be just as out of place as a gay, frolicsome approach to long division. The appropriateness of behavior is much more dependent on the purposes of the teacher than on any characteristic of the behavior itself.

In some sections of a city, a boy may carry a pocketknife to school without ever being questioned. In other schools in the same city, even nail files are confiscated as potentially dangerous weapons.

Situations like these have convinced us that it is a fruitless approach to attempt to categorize misbehavior in terms of the responses themselves. We believe that the only realistic position one can take is that any behavior is deviant if the teacher (principal, school board) deems it so.

WHAT ARE SOME DEVIANCIES TEACHERS LIST?

Even with our admission that a deviancy is what the teacher says it is, it is amusing, if not instructive to look at some lists of misbehaviors that have been compiled over the last one hundred years or so in this country. S. L. Pressey (1939) found a list of deviancies published by a North Carolina high school in 1848. Here are some of them arranged in descending order of seriousness:

1. Playing cards at school (10 lashes).
2. Swearing at school (8 lashes).
3. Drinking liquor at school (8 lashes).
4. Telling lies (7 lashes).
5. Boys and girls playing together (4 lashes).
6. Quarreling (4 lashes).
7. Wearing long fingernails (2 lashes).
8. Blotting one's copybook (2 lashes).
9. Neglecting to bow when going home (2 lashes).

The *Elementary School Journal* for October 1928 carried a list of offenses together with the punishments thought appropriate for each. Some of the items on H. W. James' list follow:

1. Truancy.
   a. Keep pupil in after school to make up work.
   b. Report case to parents.
   c. Report case to public officer.
2. The "show-off" attitude.
   a. Put offender in place by remark that will enlist pupils on your side.
   b. Removal of privileges.
   c. Public acknowledgment of fault.
3. Dishonesty in assigned work.
   a. Removal of credit.
   b. Assignment of extra work.
   c. Seat pupil apart from the group.
4. Overzealousness in recitation.
   a. Assignment of extra work.
5. Bullying.
   a. Oral reproof.
   b. Removal of privileges.

When Schrupp and Gjerde (1953) asked teachers to rate student behaviors that they currently considered to be serious, the following partial list emerged: defiance, rudeness, obscene notes and pictures, disobedience, disorderliness, heterosexual activity, masturbation, and untruthfulness.

J. E. Greene (1962) compiled the following array of alleged misbehaviors cited by the teachers of senior-high-school students. They are listed in in order of their frequency: talking, disobedience, carelessness, defiance of authority, cutting class, inattention, tardiness, cheating, and throwing objects.

In a large survey of administrators in New York and California, Duke (1978a) found that the three most pressing problems were skipping class, truancy, and tardiness. The results showed that profanity, fighting, disrespect, drug use, disruption, and smoking were all listed among their least pressing problems. These were surprising findings in the face of recent horror stories about the growing incidence of murder, rape, and assault in the schools.

WHAT INFLUENCES A TEACHER'S JUDGMENTS OF DEVIANCY?

A glance at these lists of misbehaviors and a quick perusal of your own experiences will attest to the fact that even though judgments may change with time and place, there are some startling similarities among the arrays of discipline problems educators have encountered over the years.

One way of organizing this plethora of alleged offenses consists of placing each deviancy in one of five different categories. These categories are based on the type of consideration a teacher makes when judging any action to be deviant.

Moral Considerations

At least nine of the misbehaviors listed earlier were probably judged so on the basis of their moral implications. Playing cards, swearing, drinking, lying, long fingernails, heterosexual activity, obscenity, and masturbation were all probably considered immoral by the teachers who listed them. The fact that "boys and girls playing together" was deserving of four lashes in 1848 is a startling reminder that we are forever operating under a "new morality." Unless a teacher wishes to run the risk of imposing his own ethics on the children of citizens who also have freedom of belief, he must constantly be looking for a more inclusive standard.

Though the specific items on the list may change from one time or locale to another, moral implications of behavior will no doubt remain a potent influence on teachers' disciplinary decisions.

Personal Considerations

Although all evaluations may be thought of as somewhat personal, this category is reserved for those behaviors that irk the teacher for reasons of preference unique to himself. Failure to bow, a "show-off" attitude, overzealousness in recitation, carelessness, defiance, rudeness, and disobedience all show a strong personal element behind their indictment.

Legal Considerations

This category could include both those prohibitions that are part of the state or local school law and extra-legal rules made by the administrative personnel of a building. Truancy, cutting class, and tardiness probably fall into this category.

Incidentally, Duke (1978a) found evidence that teachers and students did not always agree with administrators on what problems were most pressing. If this "perceptual dissonance" is widespread, it could account for the confusion and inconsistency surrounding school rules.

Safety Considerations

Safety considerations will almost certainly overlap the legal and moral aspects of judgment, but there may be some behaviors that are taboo principally because of their threat to the health and safety of the students. Quarreling, bullying, and throwing objects could easily fit into this category. With the advent of the high school automobile operator, drinking could be placed here also. One could realistically add the fire hazard of smoking to the list, as well as the physical and social dangers of drug use.

Educational Considerations

Only a few of the deviancies on our lists fell clearly into the category of educational considerations, although several others might have shared this designation with another. Inattention and talking would certainly impede the learning process, whereas cheating, tardiness, and truancy could be objected to on educational grounds. As with most human judgments, almost every misdeed cited could be censured for a number of reasons.

Pupil Control Ideology

The teacher's *pupil control idealogy* also appears to be a strong influence on the comparative emphasis placed on the categories we have described (Willower, Eidell, and Hoy, 1973). *Humanistic* teachers emphasize cooperative interaction, democracy, and self-control. On the other hand, *custodial* teachers focus primarily on strict order and assume the role of the autocrat who must control students in a punitive manner.

HOW CAN YOUR LIST OF RULES BE IMPROVED?

Since misbehavior is defined by the classroom teacher, the composition of his or her private list of rules is of primary importance. One experimenter (Crispin, 1966) has shown that a teacher tends to use the same proportion of disciplinary actions regardless of the class or the subject matter. If that list is enforced day after day and class after class, the nature of the rules is doubly important.

Make the List Minimal

While everyone agrees that rules are essential to an effective classroom, too many may be worse than too few. Duke (1978b) speculates that rules may sometimes even cause trouble. A case in point follows.

The recreation staff at Middle State Orphanage were at their wits' end. The weekly dance held for their teen-aged charges had become a nightmare of delinquency. Both fellows and girls seemed bent on coming to the dance in the grubbiest attire that they could find. Determined to teach them something about proper dress, the recreation leaders spent the better part of each evening insisting that the boys tuck in their shirts and that the girls must wear skirts instead of pants. Their demands were met with hostility and defiance, and the dances were hardly worth holding.

In consultation with a local psychologist, the staff decided that their grooming demands were a lot less important than the wholesome recreation they were trying to provide. They reasoned that adolescents in a state orphanage had already had more than their share of frustrations and that adding new ones should only be done where absolutely essential.

For the next month, nothing was said about shirt tails or skirts during the weekly recreation dances. Not only was the staff relieved of the necessity of spending all evening as policemen, but incidents resulting from student hostility to the rules disappeared. Several months later the group reported to the psychologist that the dances were going smoothly and the level of dress had slowly improved.

Believe it or not, Alschuler (1977) found one school with more than 100 rules on the books! If you multiply that number by 25 students, an astronomical number of violations becomes possible at any classroom moment.

A lot of effective teachers believe that a good list length is about 5 rules.

Make the List Relevant

One giant step toward reducing your list involves the purging of all those items that are not focused on learning.

This requires that a teacher have a clear idea of the objectives of the particular course or homeroom class that she or he is teaching. In terms of the considerations cited in the first part of this chapter, making a list relevant would consist of making sure that a majority of the classroom rules were firmly based on educational considerations. Chewing gum, the length of a boy's hair, the tightness of trouser hiplines, and the length of the girls' skirts—many of these might be taken off the deviancy list if a major criterion were educational relevancy.

Make the List Meaningful

In later chapters we shall refer to the beneficial effects of control techniques that are task-oriented rather than approval-oriented. If a teacher has made a list of rules that are both minimal and relevant, it should be a short, easy step to make that list meaningful to students. Rules that bear a logical relationship to the educational tasks at hand are difficult for students to write off as dictatorial caprice. Ms. Neff insisted that the students in her English class fold their papers lengthwise and place their names on the outside of the folded work. She refused to accept a paper until it was done according to proper form, but her students seldom complained. At the beginning of each semester of English, Ms. Neff took great pains to explain to the class that her system made it easy to avoid grading a student on the way she felt toward him instead of the content and mechanics of his writing.

She pointed out that if the names were put on the outside of the back of the paper, she could then unfold them all, read and grade them without looking at the name. She explained that this should result in a fairer grade for everyone.

As you know, relevance is often in the mind of the lawmaker. When that relevance has been effectively explained to the governed, meaning suddenly emerges.

Make the List Positive

In a later chapter, we will point out that a student learns proper classroom behavior by doing it and by feeling rewarded for his efforts. Although a rule may always imply its opposite, a positive statement offers a goal to work toward rather than a veiled threat to avoid.

Mr. Martin found that his elementary science students could learn a lot from one another if they conversed about the experiments they were doing at their tables. At the same time, the noise volume had sometimes risen too high for effective work. He solved this problem neatly by describing a just-above-a-whisper "science voice," which he asked his students to put on as soon as they came through the door. To insist that pupils use their "science voice" is a much more attractive way to state the rule than to declare, "There will be no loud talking in this room!"

During the high school years, when students are experimenting with independence, a "thou shall not" rule seems to be an invitation to insurrection.

Invite Student Input

Good administrators know that their teachers should be deeply involved in the process of making new policies and procedures. Effective teachers also include their students in building a set of effective rules for the classroom. Glasser (1969) even suggests periodic room meetings, in which the social problems of the class are discussed and solved.

SUMMARY AND DISCUSSION

The classroom teacher defines behavior and misbehavior by the kinds of rules that she or he makes and enforces in class. Although each teacher makes a somewhat different list, most of the lists are based on moral, personal, legal, safety, and educational considerations. The teacher's pupil-control ideology influences the weight put on each category.

If the number of disciplinary actions a teacher takes is to be diminished, a minimal list of rules is a prerequisite. The whole idea of carefully specifying a set of classroom rules is based on the expectancy component of our motivational model. Students must be certain of what behaviors are approved and will therefore be rewarded. When students understand the connection between the rules and the fulfillment of their own needs, the list becomes both relevant and meaningful. Open discussions between teachers and students can greatly facilitate this process.

Since potentially disruptive students may have low frustration tolerance, stating the "do's" rather than the "don'ts" will usually be more effective.

Having discussed the importance and procedures for setting up an effective list of rules, we move on to Chapter 6, to detail some other documented ways to prevent discipline problems from arising.

FEEDBACK QUIZ

1. In the final analysis, which of the following determines if a student's actions are deviant? (a) religion, (b) social norms, (c) the student, (d) the teacher.
2. Which of the following words most accurately compares the different lists of misbehaviors? (a) conflicting, (b) identical, (c) similar, (d) unrelated.
3. Which of the following categories includes rules about attendance? (a) legal, (b) moral, (c) personal, (d) safety.
4. Which of the following is a pupil-control ideology that is punitive? (a) custodial, (b) educational, (c) humanistic, (d) moral.
5. Which of the following characteristics of a good list of rules is most closely related to educational influences? (a) meaningful, (b) minimal, (c) positive, (d) relevant.
6. Specifying a clear set of rules has its major influence on (a) arousal, (b) expectancy, (c) punishment, (d) reward.
7. A list of rules becomes both relevant and meaningful when students perceive its relationship to their (a) arousal, (b) expectancies, (c) needs, (d) punishments.

Six

Avoiding
Misbehavior:
Classroom
Management

1. List five parts of a careful lesson plan.

2. Define the term *thought experiment* and explain why it is an important part of planning.

3. Explain how busy work may be helpful, even if a limited amount of academic learning results.

4. Describe the usual progression of classroom misbehavior from the first day of class and indicate when control is most crucial.

5. Define the term *optimal movement* and list five types of slow-downs that prevent it.

6. Describe two ways to engineer smooth transitions and list five ways they can be disrupted.

7. List and describe three techniques that keep students alert in class.

8. Describe two methods of keeping students accountable for their own schoolwork and explain how these are related to internality.

9. List and explain seven categories of variety that can be introduced into the classroom.

10. Describe four procedures that can improve your surveillance of student behavior.

11. List three characteristics of activity signal systems that can reduce student disruption and explain how a teacher can make use of each.

12. Relate each of the items above to the motivational model of human behavior.

. . . It was immediately obvious that she was going to have problems. The class of 23 boys and 7 girls was a mixture of sophomores and juniors taking U.S. History and Government.

. . . Students spoke out during the class without being recognized, engaged in *sotto voce* mockery of the teacher, arrived late for class and attempted to leave early, and began giving 'wise' answers, such as suggesting that the best way to save tax money would be to cut teachers' salaries.

By Monday of the third week of school, students were openly speaking out, talking to each other, and ignoring the teacher.

On Friday, Tim had a stack of newspapers on his desk. Mrs. Sims became irritated and put them on top of a cabinet. As she turned her back, Tim got up as if to take them back. Then he smiled, and his lips formed the words 'better not.' He sat down. Shortly thereafter, he moved to a different seat. It was at this point that Mrs. Sims decided to 'take it seriously,' and dismissed Tim from class. Another student immediately put in, 'Can I go too?' 'No, I want you to give a report to class in a few minutes,' Mrs. Sims replied. Nonetheless, the second student left. Whether this was a show of support for Tim or a way to get out of giving a report I don't know. The class 'discussion' lapsed into a monologue by Mrs. Sims and then ended (Wegmann, 1976, pp. 72, 73, 74).

HOW CAN YOU PREVENT MISBEHAVIOR?

It certainly won't surprise you to learn that the situation in Mrs. Sims' history class deteriorated even more and that her 30 students didn't learn much subject matter that semester. But was it all really necessary? Could the ensuing chaos have been prevented? Was there some point in this grim progression of events where the class could have been saved?

Plan Activities Carefully

If you haven't found out already, you will soon learn that teaching "off the top of your head" is an invitation to disaster. The experienced teacher can get away with it for a while, but only because his or her memory banks contain the results of a wide variety of informal experiments carried out in the past. But sooner or later all poorly planned teaching self-destructs.

Realizing this, teacher training institutions insist that their students spend a great deal of time writing lesson plans with a lot of rich detail. Complicated taxonomies (Bloom, 1956; Gagne, 1965) and technologies (Mager, 1962) have been developed to make sure that the objectives of instruction are both clear and precise. Planning also includes some asssessment of the readiness of the students; a description of the learning activities; a list of the necessary materials; and some way to summarize, evaluate, and make assignments for the next lesson.

Perform Thought Experiments

But one important step that the effective teacher usually adds to the planning process is the *thought experiment* (Yinger, 1977). At the point where you are deciding which of several activities you will use to meet your objectives, take time to think through how each will work in your own classroom. This mental rehearsal must include many of the elements of a dramatic production: cast, stage, props, and time.

As you think through the different scenarios, scene by scene, not only will you be able to make a more accurate judgment as to which activity you should initiate, but you will be able to anticipate potential hazards.

You may remember being the victim of a teacher who neglected to carry out thought experiments ahead of time. One young college professor came to give his first unit test to a huge lecture class of 350 students. Because he had failed to do a thought experiment, the tests were unnumbered, uncounted, unstacked, and all the same form. It took nearly half the period just to pass them out. Then because of the single form and the shoulder-to-shoulder seating arrangement, unbridled cheating was assured.

I once arranged for an elementary science class to make charming little baskets out of cockle burrs. I had found the activity in a revered nature study book and made the mistake of trying to put the plan into action without doing a thought experiment. Within 15 minutes, my second graders were milling about and scratching vigorously at angry rashes on their forearms. Some were jumping up and down in discomfort while tears began to form in the eyes of others. I began to feel the cold fingers of panic. I quickly dispatched one nonaffected student to fetch the assistant principal. She appeared at the height of the chaos and calmly directed a thorough washing and creaming regime that eventually quieted the tumult. Talk about egg on your face!

The point is that effective classroom management must be based not only on sound objectives, but on a knowledge of what is likely to work in a particular classroom environment. Thought experiments are one way to add this important ingredient.

Keep Students Occupied

While Doyle (1979) suggests that teachers perceive classrooms as units of time to be filled with educationally justifiable activities, Arlin (1979) asserts that, from a misbehavior standpoint, *filling* the time is doubly important. The following account dramatizes the point beautifully:

One student teacher had the questionable opportunity of leading a "band" practice for a group of seventh graders whose participation in band was less than voluntary (they were required to choose band or art). After the student teacher made the transition from each song to the next, each band section had to play its part. Those waiting began to occupy themselves with nonband activities. A particularly popular activity was hurling various missiles (pencils, gum, combs) across the room and into the tuba. Other activities, such as physical duelling with flutes and clarinets, were equally off-task. With the student teacher on the point of tears, the cooperating teacher returned to the room and took over, whereupon the class went smoothly. The cooperating teacher, who had a reputation for "good discipline," gave this advice in discussing the disastrous situation afterward: "Always make sure the kids have an instrument in their mouth, so they can't spit at each other, and something in their hands so they can't throw anything. Never let kids wait longer than a minute for anything. You can't bog down or you'll pay for it." In my conversations with teachers about transitions in the context of time flow, this notion reappeared frequently, although never quite so starkly [Arlin, 1979, p. 53].

It is widely agreed among experienced teachers that overplanning is much safer than underplanning. Some even include backup activities in case the main ones don't live up to expectations.

Gain Early Control

Doyle (1979) has documented the basis for the traditional "don't smile until Christmas" advice that old-timers often give to new teachers. It has been shown that after a brief honeymoon period, classroom misbehavior rises rapidly to a peak. If the teacher practices effective management skills during this critical period, deviancy falls off and levels out. If not, misbehavior rates continue to rise until the class becomes virtually unmanageable. The sad story of Mrs. Sims is a case in point.

HOW CAN YOU MANAGE MORE EFFECTIVELY?

Pioneering research on classroom management skills has been carried out by Jacob S. Kounin and his colleagues at Wayne State University. Their results were obtained from a detailed analysis of hundreds of hours of videotapes made in actual classroom settings (Kounin, 1970). This section leans heavily on that research and spinoffs of those seminal investigations that continue to appear in the literature. Momentum, smoothness, group alerting, and signal systems all appear to be important variables.

Use Momentum Skillfully

Kounin found that misbehavior incidents were significantly fewer during lessons that moved fast enough to be interesting but slowly enough not to leave students behind. When teacher actions interfered with that *optimal movement*, discipline problems began to arise. Overdwelling and fragmentation are two types of slowdowns that unnecessarily restrict the momentum of the lesson. *Behavior overdwelling* refers to teachers making a big deal out of some misbehavior a student has committed.

"You should know better than that, Ronald," glared Ms. Eckrich. "We *always* put our books away before we take a test. I have told you over and over again that your desk must be clear during a test. You should have learned that in the fourth grade and yet here you are at the end of fifth and you still haven't caught on." Ms. E's voice had now risen half an octave and the last sentence was delivered at a volume just below a shriek. "If you insist upon breaking the rules again and again, I don't see much hope for you. You will probably end up in reform school with all the other dummies who wouldn't listen to their teachers!"

By this time some of the other students were rolling their eyes. Many shifted uncomfortably in their seats. Few if any were ready for the test that was supposed to be the central activity for the day. Everyone in class paid dearly for the teacher's soapbox oration, including Ms. Eckrich.

Actone overdwelling is another slowdown that Kounin discovered. It refers to a teacher's spending too much time focusing on one small part of a larger activity. Mr. Fager had a "thing" about passing. Day after day he drilled his basketball team on the various techniques of effective passing, leaving only about a half hour for scrimmage. At the end of the second week, he had a near-mutiny to deal with. "What's the use of throwing the ball around," said one lanky forward, "if you can't even shoot the basket?"

Prop overdwelling also causes aggravating slowdowns. Sometimes teachers spend too much time explaining a piece of equipment and forget the objectives of the lesson. Ms. Garth wanted her biology students to see the Euglena in an infusion she had made. Student eagerness turned into consternation when she spent the entire period having the class draw and label the parts of the microscope they would use to do the job.

Task overdwelling refers to a slowdown that features too many directions for the activity at hand. Mr. Harold had a little verbal routine that he went through every time he gave a spelling test. He repeated it so exactly that his students couldn't tell it from a Memorex tape. "Now clear your desks of everything except your pencil and spelling tablet. Remember that we slant our books a bit to the left, not to the right, unless of course you are left-handed. Your name should be printed, not written, in the upper left-hand corner on the top line. Please number your papers from 1 to 10 in two columns, 1 to 5 in the first column and 6 to 10 in the second. I will pronounce each spelling word twice, and you should write it as neatly as possible. If you want a word defined, please raise your hand after I have pronounced it for the second time. Ready? Here we go!" After the third week of reruns, students began to show their impatience in many ways. One girl had become expert at lip-synching the act and amused everyone who saw her "speaking" in Harold's scholarly baritone.

Group fragmentation is another slowdown that disturbs a healthy class momentum. This happens when a teacher asks students to do a group activity one at a time. Ms. Ipswitch always asks five (count 'em) students to put their solutions to homework problems on the chalkboard so that the rest can check their own papers. Since she insists on solo performances, her students must wait five times as long to get the job done. Creativity in this class consists of finding innovative nonarithmetic diversions to fill up the "dead air" time.

Prop and actone fragmentation are also guilty of disrupting optimal class momentum. These result when a teacher artifically splits up the parts of any coordinated action. Mr. Jelks has his science students make scrapbooks picturing many different animals that belong to each of the phyla. For some reason he insists that all the cutting out of pictures must be done during one period, all the pasting must be done on another, and all the explanatory writing must wait until a third.

Jelks has threatened to cut out the activity althogether, since his students are so difficult to handle.

Structure Smooth Transitions

Recent research (Arlin 1979) corroborates Kounin's assertion that misbehaviors multiply during poorly structured transitions. When teachers lose track of the time and the bell rings before the lesson has been wrapped up, all hell can break loose. Students often rush out in massive disarray with their mentor shouting the next day's assignment after them.

Teachers who engineer smooth transitions not only plan well in advance but lay out the lesson for their students so that everyone knows what to expect. If time begins to run short, these smoothies deliver a two-minute warning like "Please try to finish up in a couple of minutes because then we have to get ready for gym class."

Arlin (1979) found that smooth transitions are achieved by teachers who clearly break the momentum of one activity before starting another. Somehow they also maintain the general momentum for the entire school day. But transitions can be ruined by thrusts, dangles, truncations, flip-flops, and stimulus boundedness.

Thrusts are unannounced intrusions that disturb the progress of the lesson. Ms. Gantt's third graders were finally working quietly and effectively on their social studies assignments when the writing teacher flung open the classroom door and shouted, "Are you ready yet?" Gantt loudly admitted that they hadn't practiced their penmanship yet and invited her colleague to come back later. As you can guess, social studies was in a shambles for the remainder of the period.

Mr. Banks also committed a costly thrust during a math test he was administering. Shortly after his class had dutifully begun the chore, he discovered a minor spelling error on the second page. "Stop," he bellowed, "everyone stop! I want you to turn to page two of your exam and look at the third word in the second example. It should be t-h-e-i-r, not t-h-e-r-e." He subsequently paid dearly for his failure to proofread ahead of time.

Smoothness can also be disrupted by a *dangle*, beginning one activity and then shifting to another without achieving closure on the first. "Today we're going to find out who wins the race," announced Ms. Carruthers, referring to a book she had been reading to her fourth-graders. With rapt attention her eager charges listened as she began to read animatedly about preparations for the big horse race. About halfway through the chapter Carruthers asked the class if they knew what a Palamino horse looked like. When no one raised a hand, she launched into the history of the name and breeding practices that produced such beauties. Since she was quite a horse buff, the teacher went on and on. It wasn't long until the volume of whispering, note-passing, and horseplay (no pun intended) forced her to return to the reading of the chapter. Shortly all was quiet again as the exciting narrative continued to unfold.

Ms. Carruthers had committed a bad dangle. If she had gone on about Palaminos until the end of class, Kounin would have called it a *truncation*. Both management mistakes sabotage smoothness and predictably result in disruption.

Another practice that damages smoothness has been called a *flip-flop*. Teachers who move from one topic to another and then return to the first are asking for trouble. Sam Dancey had just finished discussing the results of a unit quiz on simultaneous equations. "Now that we have finished this unit, we will begin our study of functions," he declared. About five minutes into his introduction, Dancey paused, with a faraway expression on his face.

"Did you all really understand why we got the answer we did to the fourth problem on the test?" This flip-flop was unsettling to Sam's students, and the well-known signs of restlessness soon gave him the message.

Kounin discovered some *stimulus-bounded* teachers who continually upset the smoothness of their own classes. Instead of ignoring minor distractions and responding to more salient cues, these teachers reacted to almost everything: a cough, a whisper, a dropped paper clip, a frown. In a way, they picked up and amplified dozens of intrusive stimuli that might otherwise have gone unnoticed. As a result, they were forced to spend an inordinate amount of time and energy to keep order.

Keep Students Alert

Kounin discovered that teachers who kept their students alert and accountable had significantly fewer discipline problems to deal with. Techniques that perform this group-alerting function include suspense, random recitation, recitation evaluation, and mass unison responses.

Suspense is especially effective when used in making assignments. Instead of directing her literature students to read story 23 in the anthology, Ms. Kalkins explained, "Today we will read story 23, written by O. Henry. As you read along, you will think you have the answer to the mystery, but in the last few paragraphs you will be completely astounded at the outcome!"

Kalkin's class waded right in to the assignment, hardly able to keep from reading the last paragraph first. But you must be careful not to oversell your product. If your students are continually disappointed in their assignments, they will soon brand you as a huckster and suspense will no longer be an effective tool for group alerting.

Random recitation has long been used as an effective teaching device. If students know that they can be called on at any time, they are more likely to listen and think up answers to all the questions presented. To make this technique work, you must ask your question *before* you call on a student to answer. If you say, "Bill, how many meters are there in a kilometer?" everyone else is off the hook and may not deal with the question at all.

Unless you work at it, randomness is hard to achieve. Research reveals that teachers often interact most with their better students and with those who sit "front and center" in the class (Dunkin and Biddle, 1974). One way to combat this tendency is to put student names on 3×5 cards, shuffle them, and use the resulting order to ask questions. You can pick a card off the back occasionally, so that students who have already answered won't get the idea that they are finished for the day. Some teachers make a mark on each card, indicating the quality of the answer (+ = correct; - = incorrect; ! = excellent).

Some recent research (Brophy and Putnam, 1979, p. 199) has suggested that random recitation can be overdone. It seems to be most effective when used in moderation.

Recitation evaluation is a variation on the same theme. If you ask Sally a question and she gives an answer, you can call on Emil and say, "Do you agree?" If he tries to answer with a yes or no, you should promptly ask him to explain why. Again, this rewards alertness and encourages the entire class to listen critically to all recitations.

"How many of you saw the Johnny Carson show last night?" asked Mr. Lambert. A famous authoress had been a guest, talking about her new book. Although only about one-third of the class raised their hands, this call for a *mass unison response* was quite effective as a group-alerting technique.

To accomplish the same effect, some mathematics teachers help their students make a series of cards that will fit on small individual scoreboards. As soon as the problem is presented, all students hold up their boards, indicating the results of their computations. Waiting until all scoreboards are up before going to the next problem is one way of making sure everyone has participated.

Emphasize Student Responsibility

Kounin also noted that effective teachers found ways to keep their students accountable for their learning efforts. Displays of student productions and demonstrations of their skills submit their work not only to the scrutiny of their teachers but also to the evaluation of their peers.

Bar Tal (1978) cites considerable evidence that students who have learned to take the responsibility for their own successes and failures in school usually achieve at a higher level than students who ascribe their wins and losses to luck or other outside factors beyond their control. It is reasonable to assume that misbehavior would also be reduced if students were taught to feel responsible for their own actions. We shall enlarge on ways to teach responsibility in a later chapter.

Add Lesson Variety

Since we have all experienced the deadly effects of boring assignments, it is not surprising that Kounin and his associates discovered a positive relationship between seat work variety and student behavior. Deviancy rates are low and work involvement is high during lessons that vary in content, cognitive activity, presentation, props, grouping, responsibility, and overt behavior.

Content is automatically varied in a self-contained classroom, but teachers who are with their students for only an hour at a time must work a bit harder to produce that interdisciplinary flavor. Variety in the level of cognitive ability required makes seatwork more interesting. Assignments that interweave simple fill-in-the-blank activities with situations that call for inductive and deductive reasoning are more likely to keep students on the task and off misbehavior.

Another method of adding variety to seat work is to vary the *presentation* formats. Exciting variations, such as the *Teams Games Tournaments* system (DeVries and Slavin, 1976), are welcome variations from the usual read-and-do routine.

Varying the *props* associated with assignments is an additional way to stamp out boredom. The appropriate use of tapes, computers, slides, newspapers, and teaching machines can liven up even the rote memorization and drill. The language laboratories that have been set up in many schools provide this kind of variety. Students not only listen to the language as spoken by a native but can record and play back their own attempts to duplicate the sounds.

In these days of movable desks, even *grouping* can be varied. Although parts of some assignments may require the individual to work alone, other aspects may include the combined interaction of students seated in small work groups. Because such group configurations may increase problems of surveillance and decrease the continuity of the signals, they must be used with care. We shall spell this out in greater detail later in the chapter. At any rate, changes in seating arrangements that accommodate different types of assignments can add variety and increase task involvement.

Students become impatient with assignments that spell out every detail of what they must produce. On the other hand, they may be a bit overwhelmed if their choices are unlimited. A planned alternation of the levels of student *responsibility* can bring about beneficial variety. Producing a fine piece of metal work that is within specified tolerance limits is a must for the competent industrial technology student. But an occasional opportunity to design a piece completely on one's own maintains constructive work involvement.

Assignments should give students a chance to experience a variety of different *overt behaviors*. Activities that combine writing, reading, drawing, constructing, standing, sitting, and so on are far more likely to command the interest of students than projects that are confined to any single action. Teachers have known this for ages, since one of the common forms of punishment consists of forcing students to repeat an action (write "I will be good" a thousand times) over and over again. We shall return to this unfortunate practice in a later chapter.

HOW CAN YOU MAKE BETTER USE OF SIGNALS?

Kounin's early research studies (1970) found a number of teacher actions that he called *withitness*. In the main, these actions were the result of a teacher's knowing what students were doing at all times so that prompt and appropriate action could be taken.

Subsequent investigations (Kounin and Gump, 1974; Kounin and Doyle, 1979) have revealed that the signal systems inherent in certain classroom activities have a potent influence on the level of misbehavior a teacher must deal with. It would appear that a teacher must learn to monitor appropriate student signals and also arrange for appropriate activity signals before an optimal level of control can be achieved. As we mentioned at the beginning of this chapter, the earlier a teacher can master these two procedures, the less likely it is that a class will get out of hand.

Monitor More Student Signals

Doyle (1979) has suggested several procedures that can assist a teacher in picking up student signals that call for action.

1. Arrange the seating so surveillance is easy. If students are bunched up or if objects obstruct the teacher's view, misbehavior may get a head start before it is detected.

2. Select a steering group to act as an early barometer of impending trouble. It should be made up of those individuals who are most likely to misbehave. They will let you know when to adjust the pacing and interest so that you can achieve maximum on-task behavior.

3. Scan the entire room frequently. If you allow your attention to be monopolized by one student or a small group, off-task behavior can quickly develop in other sectors of the class.

4. Look for concealment strategies. Students who are covering their mouths, whispering, hiding behind their desks, and so on are letting you know that all is not well. You should probably let these students know that you saw them, even if you decide not to make an issue of it at the time. That way, they will know immediately that they aren't getting away with anything.

Kounin (1970) found that teachers who were good at monitoring student signals were able to discipline the right deviant promptly and attend to major problems instead of being distracted by inconsequential matters.

Improve Activity Signal Systems

Learning activities with consistent signals, high insulation, and low intrusiveness are highly resistant to misbehavior problems.

Arlin (1979) found that teachers can increase the *signal consistency* by establishing routines that are frequently repeated. At the beginning of the school year, effective teachers "walk their classes through" these procedures until they have become habitual. Some even make students "start over" when they have performed a routine incorrectly.

Doyle (1979) points out that such routines may include administrative operations, recurring lessons, and instructional moves. Taking roll, passing out supplies, breaking up into groups, and moving from class to class are all examples of administrative operations that can be routinized early. Taking spelling tests, listing and defining vocabulary words, conducting reviews, and other recurring lesson formats also lend themselves to early routinization. Some instructional moves that can become routines include asking questions, praising answers, and giving directions. If routines are effectively established during the formative stage of the school year, teachers are able to give more time and attention to meaningful student signals.

With respect to *insulation*, any means of eliminating distractions can be effective. Shutting the blinds on a baseball game, closing the classroom door to eliminate hall noise, pulling down a shade to keep bright sunlight from interfering: all these are examples of insulating students from disrupting stimuli.

In order to eliminate the intrusion of classmates into one another's work, activities can be chosen that restrict pupil interaction. Individual construction projects usually produce more learner involvement than group projects of a similar nature. Listening to the teacher or a record produces much less misbehavior than promoting a class discussion. Although you might choose an interactive format for other very good reasons, you can be sure that control will be more difficult.

SUMMARY AND DISCUSSION

Research in classroom management continues to discover ways in which teachers can prevent student misbehavior. These techniques are closely related to our motivational model. Careful preplanning and thought experiments make the teacher's own expectancy more accurate. Lessons that keep students well occupied with appropriately paced, rewarding activities guard against boring intervals in which their needs are not being met.

Smooth transitions result from more accurate student expectancy. Knowledge about the lesson plans and gentle reminders about time parameters help students set realistic learning goals for the day.

Both variety and group-alerting techniques result in optimum student arousal. Increased student responsibility results when they are frequently aroused to respond and when appropriate rewards follow satisfactory performance.

As teachers become more successful in monitoring student signals, they become aroused and alert at times that are crucial to effective discipline.

When teachers establish more consistent signals, their students' expectancy is more accurate, so that they can set more realistic learning goals. When distracting stimuli are eliminated, students are more easily aroused by the lesson stimuli and their attention is more easily focused on learning.

Having described a number of ways to avoid discipline problems in the classroom, we move on to Chapter 7, in which we describe techniques for responding to those deviancies that happen anyway.

FEEDBACK QUIZ

1. Which of the following is usually *not* part of the lesson plan? (a) instructional materials, (b) learning activities, (c) specific objectives, (d) thought experiments.
2. Thought experiments improve one's (a) creativity, (b) intelligence, (c) problem-solving skills, (d) teaching effectiveness.
3. Which of the following procedures is most likely to prevent student misbehavior? (a) assessing student readiness, (b) introducing new activities, (c) keeping students busy, (d) writing precise objectives.
4. In what part of the school year does the number of student disruptions first begin to rise? (a) the first hour, (b) after a brief honeymoon period, (c) about the middle, (d) toward the end.
5. Which of the following retards the momentum of a lesson? (a) actone fragmentation, (b) dangle, (c) flip-flop, (d) thrust.
6. Which of the following interferes with smooth transitions? (a) prop overdwelling, (b) stimulus boundedness, (c) task fragmentation, (d) task overdwelling.
7. Which of the following is *not* a technique for group alerting? (a) internality, (b) mass unison responses, (c) random recitation, (d) suspense.

8. Students with an internal locus of control take responsibility for (a) their failures, (b) their successes, (c) both a and b, (d) neither a nor b.

9. Misbehavior is lower in classes that are interesting. Interest may be increased by adding (a) externality, (b) routines, (c) smooth transitions, (d) variety.

10. Selection of an appropriate steering group can improve a teacher's (a) concealment strategies, (b) insulation effect, (c) lesson signals, (d) surveillance effectiveness.

11. Signal systems in small-group discussions are high in (a) consistency, (b) insulation, (c) intrusiveness, (d) lesson involvement.

12. Keeping students busy has its major impact on the _____ aspect of motivation. (a) arousal, (b) expectancy, (c) needs, (d) punishment.

13. Variety and group-alerting techniques have their primary impact on the _____ aspect of motivation. (a) arousal, (b) expectancy, (c) needs, (d) punishment.

14. When unplanned stimuli distract students from their work, the _____ aspect of motivation is most heavily involved. (a) arousal, (b) expectancy, (c) needs, (d) punishment.

Seven

Antiseptic Control Techniques and Punishment

OBJECTIVES

1. List five outcomes of antiseptic classroom control.

2. List and describe seven antiseptic control techniques that reduce student frustration.

3. List four characteristics of a situation in which a teacher should probably ignore a misbehavior.

4. Illustrate seven techniques that restore order by activating positive student motives.

5. Explain why *protective restraint* is difficult to keep antiseptic.

6. Define punishment and list four different kinds.

7. List and explain four destructive side effects of physical punishment.

8. Explain why verbal punishment may produce some of the same side effects as physical punishment.

9. Define *response cost* and explain how its effects compare to physical and verbal punishment.

10. List six ways to increase the effectiveness of punishment and explain why each works.

11. Relate each of the items above to the motivational model of human behavior.

Mr. Poole was at his wits' end again. It was just far enough along on a Friday afternoon that he had begun to relax and let his mind go through its weekly T.G.I.F. routine. It had been one thing after another that week at Peerless Junior High. Broken windows had greeted them on Monday morning; the washrooms had been flooded on Wednesday; yesterday was the rescheduling nightmare that always went with the taking of class and individual pictures; and now this on Friday afternoon.

Mr. Slater, the custodian, came puffing in from servicing a girls' washroom between the fifth- and sixth-hour classes. Lowering his voice to a hoarse whisper so that the school secretary could not overhear, he described in lurid detail a message he had found written on the wall in Purple Passion lipstick. The inscription was well laced with code-negative, four-letter words, and Mr. Slater's grim expression belied the twinkle in his eyes as he went over the words for the fifth time.

Mr. Poole was about to do his administrative duty and go down to view the evidence, but the energetic custodian assured him that he had scrubbed the message off immediately, so that no one else would have to look at such filth. It was at that moment that a plan occurred to the harried principal.

Throwing on the intercom switches, he broke into all the seventy-five sixth-hour classes with a "now hear this" that would have made any boatswain jealous. In one minute, every student and teacher in the building knew that someone had written an obscene note in the girls' restroom. They knew that Mr. Poole wanted the culprit to turn herself in before the end of the hour. They were also informed that no one would receive class pictures the next week until the mystery was solved and the criminal apprehended.

As you can well imagine, not much learning took place at Peerless during the remainder of the afternoon. There was an undertone of nervous conversation in every class. Notes flitted silently back and forth across the rooms. Petitions of protest against mass punishment were already being worded in the minds of some of the young rebels, and requests for passes to the girls' washrooms increased 50 percent above the normal number.

Between sixth and seventh hours, the girls' lavatories were so crowded that several girls were late to their last class. Although Mr. Poole had not said which washroom was the scene of the crime, every girl thought it might be the one on her floor. Every tile on every wall within reach was gone over with the thoroughness of the FBI for some trace of the intriguing message, but not so much as a smudge of Purple Passion lipstick was unearthed. As the day ended, the culprit had not come forth; thus the drama would have to be continued the next week.

Three days of the next week went by, and the mystery still had not been solved. Pictures were to be handed out on Thursday, but daily reminders on the intercom assured the students that they would be withheld until June if necessary. Then somebody "finked."

A girl who had entered the lavatory just as the author of the obscenity was leaving told what she knew to the principal, and the criminal was apprehended, Purple Passion lipstick and all.

Boatswain Poole came back on the intercom and informed all seventy-five classes that the malefactor had been caught and that pictures would be passed out on schedule. After assuring the students that the girl would be expelled, he complimented them on the fine citizenship shown by the majority and said he was sorry that a few delinquents had to make it so hard on the rest of the school.

WHAT ARE SOME OUTCOMES OF EFFECTIVE CONTROL?

In judging the advisability of using the kinds of techniques employed by Mr. Poole, we must set down some guidelines for evaluation.

There are those who will read the incident and conclude immediately that it was a good move because it worked. What they mean is that the deviant was apprehended and punishment was meted out. But as we shall see, there are several additional outcomes to be desired.

The Misbehavior Ceases

It almost goes without saying that, in order to be effective, a control technique must put an end to the misbehavior. Not only must an optimum learning atmosphere be promptly restored, but, as we pointed out in Chapter 6, uncontrolled students eventually become unmanageable. In the lipstick obscenity case, the deviancy *did* cease. Of course it had already ceased when the culprit walked out the door, but it did not recur that year. The point to remember is that cessation is not the only desirable outcome of a control technique.

Contagion Is Limited

There is pitifully little consolation in the fact that you have stopped one culprit, only to discover that your methods have made deviants out of the remainder of the class. Whenever a control technique is used on one disruptive student, it influences the classroom audience vicariously. Gnagey (1960) has shown that this *ripple effect* is particularly strong when the deviant is a class leader. The point is that your success or failure in disciplining one student influences the behavior of all the others.

Effective Relationships Persist

Redl and Wattenberg (1959) suggest that before deciding how to handle a deviancy, one should consider a two-pronged question:

How will it affect the deviant's relationship with his or her classmates and with the teacher?

It would hardly do to gain the control and lose the student. As peer relationships are so important in the psychological life of a student, and as problems in this area can most certainly inhibit the educational process, any control technique that appreciably decreases a deviant's status in the eyes of classmates may trigger more problems than it solves.

Similarly, there are a lot of tomorrows to be considered, which will include the teacher's continued relationship with the deviant. Long after everyone has forgotten just what happened, the teacher and the deviant must interact in such a way that optimum learning will take place. If a control technique is selected that is too harsh or unfair, a deviant may become so angry or afraid that a constructive relationship with the teacher may be virtually impossible from that time on.

In the lipstick case, human relations were not maintained. Aside from the anguish that the deviant and her parents may have gone through during her period of banishment, we can be glad that Mr. Poole was not a classroom teacher. He would then have had to face the daily outrage of students who were to have been punished for someone else's misbehavior.

Learning Efficiency Increases

Although certainly not separate from other considerations, a control technique should improve the chances that learning will take place. If deviancies are occurring in profusion, these multiple distractions cannot help but cut down educational efficiency (Gnagey, 1960). An equally unfortunate situation arises when the control technique a teacher uses disrupts the learning atmosphere to a greater extent than the deviancy. In the lipstick case, learning actually became less efficient. Not only were all seventy-five sixth-hour classes sabotaged by Principal Poole's intercom ultimatum, but the disrupted feelings of the students inhibited learning for nearly a full week. His continued warnings over the loudspeaker were hardly neutralized by his final admission that most of the students were good citizens.

Someone has said that the kindergarten or nursery-school teacher is the most important figure in public education, because he or she sets the stage for the next twelve years of schooling. Actually, every teacher adds to or detracts from students' love of learning. The emotional responses that the teacher helps classes to associate with school and the learning process may be as important as the subject matter that the teacher had taken so many pains to present.

Control techniques that continually elicit negative feelings from deviants and their classmates do their part in building up a host of emotional barriers to further learning. You may remember that in Chapter 4 we cited teacher aftertaste as one cause of deviancy that may be transferred from one classroom to another.

Although the fact that this control technique was carried out by a principal rather than a classroom teacher may have somewhat diluted the effect, learning *did not* gain any positive affect from this experience. Aside from the bitter feelings that the deviant was sure to have toward school, numerous students in the seventy-five classrooms at Peerless chalked it up as just one more proof that school was "for the birds," strengthening their resolve to take advantage of the opportunity to quit when they reached sixteen.

Although we can readily sympathize with Principal Poole and realize that this reaction to the lipstick note was largely the result of the multiple frustrations of an impossible week, he would probably have been better off ignoring the whole incident. One such note, quietly scrubbed off, could hardly jeopardize either the educational or moral excellence at Peerless Junior High. It almost certainly could not stir up as much consternation as the techniques employed by the harassed principal during those two weeks.

WHAT ARE SOME FUNCTIONS OF CONSTRUCTIVE CONTROL TECHNIQUES?

Redl and Wattenberg (1959) have characterized constructive control techniques as *antiseptic*. These actions get the job done without a lot of destructive side effects. In other words, constructive control techniques conform to all the guidelines we have just set up. They can be grouped into several types, according to the specific function they perform.

Some Reduce Frustration

You will remember that we pointed out in earlier chapters that deviancy may be a reaction to frustration. Though an obvious remedy for such situations is the removal of those frustrating situations, it is helpful to spell out some specific ways in which this must be done.

The use of *diagnostic pretests* is one way to eliminate some subject-matter frustrations before they arise. With all our talk about individual differences and readiness and "beginning where the child is," there are a startling number of teachers who "just start teaching." A practice like this spells frustration almost by definition.

Often an old unit final examination can be used as a diagnostic pretest. Two or three items can be selected to measure skills or knowledge in each of the several portions of the unit to come. Analysis of these results not only will show the aspects of the unit that will need the most emphasis for the whole class, but will point out specific weaknesses of each student. If the results show a lack of background in some crucial area, homework assignments or special remedial help can be started immediately to forestall greater frustration and failure further along.

Redl and Wattenberg (1959) insist that some helping over hurdles will become necessary at times, even in the best-diagnosed classes. They point out that if a student becomes unruly because of his inability to perform some part of the assignment, the teacher's point of attack should be to help with the problem rather than to make an issue out of the misconduct.

Ms. Blake came to Prim Elementary School to teach music. She had begun in the sixth grade to teach several of the popular songs from recent family movies and records. The classes were responding well and Ms. Blake was congratulating herself on having made this move.

In order to help her classes read music better, she decided to have them practice singing numbers assigned to each note so that they could get the idea of chords and intervals. Playing a three-note chord on the piano, the students were instructed to sing 1-3-5-3-1, and so on, but only a handful sang at all.

Interpreting their lack of response as impudence, Ms. Blake gave them a severe lecture about listening to instructions. She reminded them that they had done this for two years and could certainly perform better than that. When a boy in the front row raised his hand, the teacher informed him that they were here to learn music and not to talk.

After several more disheartening attempts to sing the numbers, nervous giggles and talking began to increase in the back rows. Ms. Blake went bravely on, raising her voice a bit to drown out the talkers. The gigglers in turn raised their volume, until the teacher could take it no longer. Singling out the two boys who had been talking the loudest, she sent them to the principal's office with a note stating that they had been terribly rude and unruly and that she didn't want them back in class until they had apologized.

Mercifully, the bell rang and the sixth graders filed out on tiptoe. Ms. Blake retired to the teachers' lounge in a state of angry frustration. Finding a sympathetic colleague already there, she poured out her tale of woe. She was red-faced when she heard the other teacher's response.

The music teacher who had just retired had been working with the children for two years on their sight-reading skills. Unfortunately, she had always used the syllable system. If Ms. Blake had asked them to sing do-me-sol-me-do to her chord, she might have been pleasantly surprised.

In this case, a little diagnosis would have gone a long way toward making her first few weeks more pleasant. If she had recognized the hand in the front row as a plea for hurdle help, much of the misbehavior might have been averted.

When one television program becomes uninteresting, even a first grader knows to *change the channel*. But all too often the teacher ignores the signs of boredom that indicate the lesson he or she has planned is not going well. It is as though a change in the structure of the plan would be an admission of failure and as though it is some index of valor to plod through the remainder of the lesson, no matter what.

Mr. Barnes had been droning on for some time about the Frasch process for mining sulphur. He had covered the economic values of the product, the machinery used, and the properties of this non-metal that made the process possible. He was suddenly aware that the class was not with him. Some were looking out of the window, some were passing notes, some were talking together covertly, and others were openly dozing. Realizing that it was time to "change the channel" through which the learning was supposed to be taking place, Mr. Barnes abruptly stopped his lecture and announced, "As you know, you are going to have to pass a test on this unit in a few days. One of the best ways to study for a test is to pretend that you are going to make out the exam and go through the text, making up your own questions. In the next ten minutes, I would like each of you to go through the text description of the Frasch process and make up at least three questions that you would ask if you were making out the exam. When you finish we will see if you can stump the rest of us."

Chemistry 1 suddenly came to life. Pencils were picked up. Books were opened. Notebooks became functional. Talking and note-passing deviancies ceased abruptly. Not only was there optimum participation for the rest of the period, but on the end-of-the-week quiz, it was obvious that most of the students understood the Frasch process. Redl and Wattenberg (1959) would call this *restructuring the situation.*

Temptation removal is another technique that may forestall classroom deviancies. Redl and Wineman (1957) noted that their ego-damaged boys at Pioneer House were easy prey to *gadgetorial seduction.* Although the self-control of average children may be somewhat stronger, keeping tempting objects at a minimum will reduce a lot of the conflict-frustration basic to deviancy.

Lunch money that is locked up doesn't get stolen as often as money left unattended. Displays of artifacts that are placed some distance from desks aren't as likely to be a distraction or to disappear or be broken. Checking playthings at the teacher's desk until after school may avert many distracting deviancies during the day. This certainly squares with the research on *signal insulation* that we referred to in Chapter 6.

Routines may sound like deviancy producers instead of control techniques. We often think of rules and regulations as additions to frustration instead of methods for reducing it. But a whole host of frustrations may arise just because a student has some pressing need that he cannot communicate to the teacher or that he cannot take care of himself. Routines are merely approved ways of satisfying needs that commonly arise in the classroom.

Raising one's hand to signify the wish to speak is a way of averting the frustrations of either remaining silent or shouting others down. Having a lavatory pass is a way of facilitating a child's need to go to the bathroom when he could not even politely break into the teacher's interactions with other children. Passing paper, sharpening pencils, collecting notebooks can all be organized into routines that produce minimal frustration. Cellar (1951) found that teachers who had a well-worked-out set of routines had significantly fewer disciplinary problems. As we pointed out in Chapter 6, routines also provide time for the new teacher to monitor more classroom signals.

When the demands of a situation are too much for a student for the moment, he should have some approved method of *strategic retreat*. Abbie was humiliated. She and Liz had begun laughing in the hall between classes, and now she couldn't stop. Everything seemed funny, and just when she thought she had regained control, Liz would catch her eye and it would begin all over again. People were beginning to look at her now, and the teacher was beginning to get annoyed. Abbie tried all the tricks she knew to mask her glee. She bit her lip; she pretended to be blowing her nose when she had to snicker; she told herself sternly not to be such a "jerk." But nothing helped. In the middle of an uncontrollable giggle, she suddenly realized that she had better get to the lavatory quickly or it would be too late. Abbie was embarrassed to death.

Somewhere outside the prison of her agonizing mirth, she heard Ms. Good's welcome perscription, "Abbie, we won't get any social studies learned until you get over your giggles. Why don't you go over to the girls' lounge and pull yourself together. Come back whenever you are ready." Redl and Wattenberg (1959) point out that it is important that this be a "nonpunitive exile" with the emphasis on "getting over it" rather than implied incarceration "until you can behave."

A *practice alert* can often forestall deviancies when the actual situation is encountered. The well-practiced fire drills are a fine example of this control technique. When all the moves are planned ahead so that each class knows the routine, situations seldom develop into panic, even when the alert is a real one.

Mr. Olson had arranged to take his science class through the local milk cannery. Two weeks before the field trip was to take place, he walked through the tour with the guide who was to show them around. The teacher not only made a list of important things to look for, but he also noted potential dangers such as steam pipes, unshielded machinery, and steep stairways. The class was so well briefed by the day of the trip that the experience came off without a hitch.

Comic relief often saves the day when other control techniques would only make matters worse. Movie producers usually break up prolonged suspenseful situations with the antics of some "clown." A good laugh reduces the tension enough for the audience so that as the story approaches its climax, the suspense doesn't become too uncomfortable. Damico and Purkey (1978) propose that classroom clowns may exert an extremely constructive influence on their instructional groups.

Mr. Vlasic was trying to prepare his debate squad for the county tournament. In order to motivate his affirmative team to sharpen up their case, he had just delivered the rebuttal for the negative team and completely devastated the presentation of the opposition. Furious at having been made a fool of, one of the boys on the affirmative team began to shout his outrage at the coach. Completely forgetting himself in the heat of his resentment, the irate lad referred to his teacher as a "stupid old man."

There was a dead silence as the whole team held their breath. Even the young attacker was shocked by what he had said. After a second or two of contemplation, Mr. Vlasic smiled, "Well, now that we've got me classified, let's get on with the practice."

A gale of relieved laughter followed and the debate proceeded. Afterward a grateful young debater apologized appreciatively to an understanding coach.

The beneficial effects of *catharsis* are well known in clinical circles and can be nicely applied to the classroom. Whenever it is evident that a great deal of hostility has been built up by the multiple frustrations of a school program, a teacher can arrange for what Wattenberg and Redl (1959) call "irritability drain-off." Games such as "bombardment" or "dodgeball" perform this function admirably, since a great deal of hostility can be released in a way that is neither antisocial nor dangerous. Teachers without benefit of gym equipment might hold gripe sessions in which irate students are encouraged to air their grievances. This latter method takes careful handling, however, since real catharsis often goes beyond the bounds of acceptable discussion of issues and too easily becomes focused on personalities.

Diagnostic pretests, hurdle help, changing the channel, temp-

tation removal, routines, comic relief, and *catharsis* are all constructive control techniques that avoid, reduce, or remove deviancy-causing frustrations from the classroom.

Some Trigger Positive Motives

Although there are times and places when any teacher might scoff at this assertion, most children want to be "good" most of the time. If this were not so, blackboard jungles would have overgrown the public schools long ago, and the great American dream of free education for all would have disappeared in the tangle. Not only have students learned to behave, but they have learned a healthy respect for the fact that education in these times is a *sine qua non* for the good life. The following control techniques are based on these facts and are aimed at activating the positive motivation already present within most students.

As we suggested earlier concerning Mr. Poole's handling of the lipstick incident, *ignoring* a momentary breach of conduct may often be the most constructive control technique a teacher can employ. Additional considerations that might indicate ignoring as the best policy are the following:

1. The misconduct may not be serious or dangerous.
2. The deviant may be generally well behaved.
3. Calling attention to the event might destroy the learning atmosphere.
4. The deviant will probably not be rewarded by classmates for his misdeed.

Ms. Tasher was holding a very successful discussion of the reign of Ghengis Khan in ancient Cathay. The class had read a portion of Marshall's *Caravan to Xanadu* (1953) and were eagerly comparing this account of Marco Polo's book adventures with that of the history text. Out of the corner of her eye, the history teacher noticed that Nancy Kim was busily manicuring and polishing her nails in the back row. As this practice had been specifically outlawed in the high school, a decision had to be made.

Ms. Tasher quickly decided to ignore the incident this time, and the class went on without interruption until the ringing of the bell snatched the students back from Cathay to the more mundane routines of the school schedule.

Visual prompting is also effective in reactivating a student's wish to behave properly. In cases where ignoring a deviancy seems inappropriate or inadvisable, a teacher may still handle a deviancy with signals that help bring the deviant back to the business at hand without gathering an audience.

Ms. Corda taught history at Junction High School. As is often the case, her assignment included two hours each day in which she was in charge of study hall. Whereas many of the other study-hall teachers would use this time to correct papers or read at the front desk, Ms. Corda wandered slowly from place to place, surveying the situation from many angles. Whenever two students began a conversation, the teacher moved into a position where she could catch their eye. Usually a shake of her head or a motion with her hands was enough to break up the potential study hazard. Students who were already preparing their lessons were usually completely oblivious of the incident.

Motivational recharging may be necessary when interest in a project seems to be waning and boredom begins to override self-control. This is a time when the teacher can look over the progress a student has made and reemphasize the importance of the venture.

Ms. Jackson had assigned to Jill and Marsha the job of stuffing play announcements into envelopes and addressing them to the parents of the drama class. In the meantime the cast was rehearsing some of the more difficult parts of the second act. After preparing about ten envelopes, the two girls were beginning to interfere with the rehearsal. They giggled inappropriately when close girl friends acted out tense moments, in an effort to make them forget their lines.

At the end of one of the scenes, the teacher gave instructions to the cast about setting up for the next act. She strode back to Jill and Marsha and made the following observation, "You girls will certainly have to hurry if you are going to finish the rest of these before five. Remember, if they aren't addressed and in the mail by five, they won't get to your parents in time for them to come to the play." The girls returned to their task with renewed vigor, and the rehearsal of the next act went off without an incident.

Redl and Wattenberg (1959) suggest that *defining the limits* may enable students who are already motivated to be "good" to avoid stumbling over a rule that they did not know existed. You will remember that in Chapter 7 we pointed out that "trying out the teacher" was one way students have of finding out what the rules of the game actually are.

Even for a group of students who are motivated to learn without unnecessary deviancy, it is often advisable to help them *make connections* between their behavior and its causes or consequences. Not only does this amplify the feedback that is so necessary for them to judge the appropriateness of their actions, but it can go a long way toward helping students understand their own behavior and that of their peers.

Mr. Nagy was having a hard time keeping several members of his swimming class from running on the wet concrete around the pool. One day after he had had to speak sharply to several students, he called a number of the deviants over to a patch of concrete that had just been hosed off. He explained how much more slippery it was than the dry sidewalk outside the school. He then related a true story about a student who had suffered a brain concussion several years before as a result of a serious fall near the pool. At the end of the story, Mr. Nagy emphasized the walk rule again and explained why he had to be very strict in enforcing it. From that time on, running on the deck decreased greatly.

A *post mortem* session is often useful after a deviancy has been committed. It gives the teacher a chance to help a student see the causes for his misbehavior and avoid them in the future. Care must be taken to prevent this technique from turning into an "I told you so" session aimed at vindicating the teacher's unerring judgement.

Jerry Short was crying and holding his knee. Blood was oozing out of a nasty floor burn, and the child was in obvious pain. Ms. Parsons' fourth graders had just lined up for their lavatory break, and a mad rush toward the door had resulted in Jerry's being shoved down on one knee. An old hand at such mishaps, Ms. Parsons sent a friend to help Jerry get to the school nurse. She then calmly helped the class proceed through their lavatory time. After the class returned and Jerry came back from the nurse, the teacher helped her students talk the incident over. They all agreed that they didn't want others to get hurt, and that something had to be done to improve the lining-up procedure. After a little discussion, it was decided that if one row at a time lined up, there would be less chance of mishaps. The group also reaffirmed their intent to walk into line, because running could cause a bad accident.

Ignoring, visual prompting, recharging, defining limits, making connections, and *post mortem sessions* are all techniques that are based on the assumption that most students are motivated to learn in a nondeviant manner most of the time. The function of these techniques is to activate constructive motives already learned by the students. They cannot be expected to be effective in situations where students have learned to be antiteacher, antischool, or anti-learning.

Some Impose Restraint

Although the previous section dealt with methods of behavior control, it was limited to making use of controls already internalized by most students. As there are always some pupils who cannot or will not behave themselves in school, external controls must sometimes be used to reduce disruptive misbehavior. With this procedure more than any other, it is difficult to follow the guidelines set up at the beginning of this chapter so that control will remain antiseptic.

Protective restraint is sometimes necessary when a student loses his temper and aggresses against other students. In Chapter 4, when Mr. Grange held Larruping Larry until he calmed down, the external controls were forceful but still antiseptic. Larry was being protected from hurting himself, and his classmates were being protected from Larry. It was only when the teacher began to scold and threaten that he departed from his antiseptic role. As we indicated there, this control is possible only when the teacher is much larger and stronger than the student. It differs radically also from a case in which a high school teacher is called upon to defend himself against the fists or weapons of one of his students.

HOW CAN PUNISHMENT BE USED EFFECTIVELY?

Although the techniques discussed in the first part of this chapter are usually antiseptic, the methods of punishment we will now describe are often pathogenic. When a teacher punishes a student, the teacher deliberately inflicts discomfort or pain on that pupil in the hope of suppressing some undesirable behavior. Although physical (corporal) punishment is perhaps the most controversial method, verbal flailings, fines, and withdrawal of affection are also widely applied.

Avoid Physical Punishment

In a short history of corporal punishment in American schools, Raichle (1978) notes that although growing humanitarianism has tended to discourage physical punishment, school floggings have increased alarmingly in the past ten years. This same ambivalence is evidenced by the U.S. Supreme Court, since it has upheld due process for students in disciplinary procedures but has simultaneously refused to outlaw corporal punishment in the schools. In a recent survey of the literature, Parke (1977) argues that in spite of evidence that physical punishment is still widely used in naturalistic situations, it is usually unjustified, undesirable, and unnecessary. The following side effects make corporal punishment a risky procedure at best.

1. *It sets a bad example.* It is well known that violent models, even on TV, incite aggressive behaviors in their young viewers. It is also apparent that abused children tend to become abusing parents. Even if caning a student successfully suppresses his or her obnoxious behavior, the teacher is demonstrating how to use physical aggression against another with whom he or she disagrees.

2. *It results in avoidance of the teacher.* Redd, Morris, and Martin (1975) have convincingly demonstrated that even five-year-olds learn to avoid punitive adults and prefer positive ones. In the teaching-learning situation, where teacher-student interaction is paramount, continual punishment can only reduce the effectiveness of this interpersonal process. In addition, since physical punishment usually elicits strong negative emotions, it may condition a student to feel angry or afraid of other aspects of the learning situation. This could include the subject, the physical classroom environment, and fellow students. In these times when survival depends more

and more on our continual learning of new skills and knowledge, such punishment-inspired attitudes could be devastating.

3. *Anger is often displaced on the innocent.* Our description of the despot in Chapter 3 includes a graphic account of how the accumulated anger of oft-punished students can explode into vandalism and aggravated assault. It is as though they cannot bear the whole brunt of the onslaught, but must spread it around among many others. When this happens, the effectiveness of the classroom is even further sabotaged.

4. *Creativity is throttled.* Continual physical punishment for mistakes may virtually eliminate innovative thought. Students quickly learn to focus their cognitive powers on "what the teacher wants" instead of risking the exploration of something new. If one of the functions of the young is to bring a fresh approach to the perennial problems of humankind, physical punishment can be one of the most regressive forces against progress.

Yelling, threatening, ridicule, nagging, and so on are all forms of *verbal punishment* that are often used in the classroom. Although there is very little research on the comparative effects of the different forms, it is probable that the negative side effects of verbal punishment are very similar to those of physical punishment, since they both feature a direct assault on the student.

Response cost, the levying of various types of fines, can also be effective in suppressing inappropriate behavior in the classroom. The taking away of tokens, privileges, and preferred activities may produce the desired effect without producing the destructive consequences of physical punishment. Parke (1977) points out that the withdrawal or withholding of affection can be added to the list of more tangible fines.

Emphasize Nurturant Relationships

A large number of people join the teaching profession in response to a strong need to help others. But there is always the nagging fear that a warm, caring attitude will be interpreted as weakness and may be followed by student insurrection. Not so!

Both Sears (1957) and Parke and Walters (1967) have provided evidence that a warm, affectionate relationship between teacher and students can make punishment more effective if it becomes necessary.

Perhaps you can remember the terrible remorse you felt about disappointing a teacher that you admired and liked so much. The actual punishment that you endured was far less noxious than the agonizing guilt you already felt. You may even have welcomed the punishment as one way of making up for your unfortunate transgression. I can remember being moved to offer an unsolicited apology before total expiation was mine.

Punish Early

When punishment works, it is because the unpleasant experience (or fear of it) becomes associated with the misbehavior. For this reason, the more immediate the punitive action, the better. The effectiveness of punishment decreases in direct proportion to its delay. In fact, if punishment is even delayed until the misdeed is done, then the fear may occur only after the crime has been committed. If punishment is applied early in the sequence, then a student may be afraid to go further. This effect has been demonstrated by a number of investigators (Walters, Parke, and Cane, 1965; Aronfreed and Reber, 1965; Parke and Walters, 1967; Cheyne and Walters, 1969).

In cases where punishment must be delayed for a considerable period of time, the one being punished should be verbally reminded of the behavior that led to the penalty. Psychologically, this will make sure that the punishment is associated with the unacceptable behavior.

Punish Consistently

It has been almost axiomatic among experienced teachers that consistency is the watchword of effective rule enforcement. Teachers who punish talking out one day and allow verbal free-for-alls the next are establishing a classroom roulette wheel where students take daily gambles on the outcome of their disruptive behavior. Parke (1977) refers to this as *intra-agent inconsistency*.

Sociological field studies of criminals have revealed highly erratic parental punishment patterns to be antecedent to their delinquency (Glueck and Glueck, 1950; McCord, McCord, and Howard, 1950). Laboratory studies have also confirmed these findings (Parke and Deur, 1972; Deur and Parke, 1970).

Interagent inconsistency can apparently inhibit the effectiveness of punishment (Parke, 1977). If a student interacts with four teachers who do not enforce the same basic set of rules, each of their efforts may be less effective, even if each one is consistent in his or her own classroom (Parke and Swain, 1975b; Stouwie, 1972). It appears that a principal might make a significant contribution to overall school order by facilitating some initial staff agreements about what constitutes approved and disapproved student behavior.

Use Moderate Intensity

A number of studies have shown that the effectiveness of a punishment increases with its intensity (Parke and Walters, 1967; Cheyne and Walters, 1969; Parke, 1969). Others have revealed that if the intensity is too high, some types of learning may be inhibited (Aronfreed and Leff, 1963). A third research group has noted the disruptive effects of loud verbal reprimands on the classmates of target offenders (O'Leary, Kaufman, Kass, and Drabman, 1970).

Until more evidence is in, teachers should probably use moderately intense punishment for serious offenses and try to administer it in a way that does not inhibit the learning of innocent classmates.

Provide a Rationale

Parke (1977) summarizes numerous studies that indicate reasoning to be a powerful influence on the effects of punishment. When teachers explain why they are administering a punishment, other factors such as timing, intensity, and student-teacher relationship appear to be overpowered. This is especially true when the rationale is properly matched to the cognitive development of the one being punished.

Explain Acceptable Alternatives

Pure punishment may suppress an inappropriate behavior, but it certainly does not help the deviant find other methods of fulfilling his or her needs. Walters and Parke (1967) found that punishment is much more effective if teachers explain other prosocial behavior that could be substituted for the forbidden action. To go one step further, Aronfreed (1968) points out that these suggested alternatives not only help the errant student to avoid punishment in the future, but also make it likely that he or she will get positive social reinforcement in its place.

Change Punishments Occasionally

A number of studies show that punishments lose their effectiveness over time and that new punishments are often better than older ones (Solomon, 1964; Church, 1963; Azrin, 1959, 1960; Azrin and Holy, 1961; Miller 1960). It appears that students become bored with the same old penalties just as they do with the same old learning activities.

SUMMARY AND DISCUSSION

Effective control stops the misbehavior but at the same time limits contagion, preserves human relationships, improves the learning climate, and evokes a balance of positive student emotions.

Such techniques are antiseptic because they use the elements of motivation in a constructive way. Those that reduce frustration and trigger constructive motives promote student need satisfaction in the learning context. Protective restraint keeps overwrought students from punishing themselves or their classmates in the school situation.

Since punishment activates strong safety needs, the defensive behavior that follows is often detrimental to the learning situation. Feelings of fear, anxiety, and resentment may even cause further misbehaviors.

When a positive, nurturant relationship exists between the teacher and the student, punishment is doubly effective. The misbehavior is not only suppressed by the noxious stimulus but also by the perceived loss of the teacher's regard.

Penalties should be exacted early in the misbehavior sequence and at a moderately high intensity. This suppresses the beginnings of misbehavior, so that any rewards that might have been realized at its completion do not materialize. The intensity makes a significant impact on the student's arousal and expectancy, so that contemplating future misbehavior triggers strong safety needs.

Explaining the reasons for punitive action and suggesting alternative, acceptable behaviors helps students understand how to fulfill their needs without running the risk of further punishment.

The longer a specific punishment is used, the less effective it becomes. A variety of penalities has more impact on a student's arousal.

Now that we have discussed a variety of control techniques and punishments, we turn to ways of retraining students who cause discipline problems. Chapter 8 details some successful systems of behavior modification that increase self-control.

FEEDBACK QUIZ

1. Which of the following is *not* an outcome of antiseptic control? (a) contagion is limited, (b) fear of misbehaving increases, (c) learning efficiency increases, (d) positive human relations persist.

2. Which of the following control techniques reduces frustration? (a) defining limits, (b) establishing routines, (c) making connections, (d) visual prompting.

3. Which of the following is a good reason to ignore a misbehavior? (a) a control technique would spoil a good learning activity, (b) the deviant is always in trouble, (c) the deviant will be rewarded by his or her classmates, (d) the misconduct is dangerous.

4. Which of the following techniques can be used to activate positive student motives? (a) changing the channel, (b) comic relief, (c) hurdle help, (d) post mortem sessions.

5. Which of the following control techniques is the most difficult to keep antiseptic? (a) catharsis, (b) ignoring, (c) making connections, (d) protective restraint.

6. Which of the following is *not* an example of punishment? (a) affection withdrawal, (b) paddling, (c) protective restraint, (d) threatening.

7. Which of the following is *not* a side effect of the teacher's use of physical punishment? (a) fosters displaced anger, (b) models acceptable behavior, (c) promotes teacher avoidance, (d) reduces creativity.

8. Which of the following types of punishment is most likely to have negative side effects? (a) affection withdrawal, (b) protective restraint, (c) response cost, (d) verbal.

9. Which of the following adds affection withdrawal to any other punishment a teacher may use? (a) consistency, (b) high intensity, (c) nurturant student-teacher relationships, (d) promptness of punishment.

10. Which of the following characteristics of punishment may disrupt discriminative learning? (a) consistency, (b) high intensity, (c) novelty, (d) promptness.

11. Control techniques that reduce student frustration primarily influence the _____ aspect of motivation. (a) arousal, (b) expectancy, (c) needs, (d) punishment.

12. Protective restraint impacts the _____ component of motivation. (a) arousal, (b) expectancy, (c) needs, (d) punishment.

13. Punishment activates which of the following student needs? (a) belonging, (b) esteem, (c) safety, (d) survival.

14. When the intensity of punishment is moderately high, it has more of an impact on the student's _____ and expectancy. (a) arousal, (b) needs, (c) reward.

15. Punishments used too often lose their effectiveness because of their lack of impact on student (a) arousal, (b) expectancy, (c) needs, (d) reward.

Eight

Teaching Discipline and Self-control: Behavior Modification

1. List and describe six steps in the use of behavior modification in the classroom.

2. Define and illustrate each of the following terms: *operational definition, baseline, modeling, positive reinforcement, Premack principle, extinction, time out, response cost, feedback.*

3. Describe each of the following techniques and show how the six steps of behavior modification are illustrated in each: daily report card, principal game, workclock, game machine, good behavior contract, token economy, student behavioral engineers.

4. Define the term *self-control* as it is described by Kanfer.

5. List the four components of self-management and explain how each is related to behavior modification.

6. List and illustrate five different varieties of cognitive intervention that a teacher can use to strengthen student self-control.

7. Define and illustrate the use of positive attribution to strengthen student self-control. Explain why it is superior to persuasion.

8. List and describe four ways that punishment can be made more effective in increasing student self-control.

9. Explain how behavior modification is related to our model of human motivation.

10. Relate cognitive interventions and positive attribution to our motivational model.

Jess's eighth-grade teachers found him frightening. Only 14 years old, he already weighed a powerful 185 pounds. He was easily the school's best athlete, but he loved fighting even more than he loved sports. His viciousness equaled his strength: he had knocked other students cold with beer bottles and chairs. Jess's catalog of infamy also included a 40-day suspension for hitting a principal with a stick, and an arrest and a two-and-a-half-year probation for assault.

Inevitably, Jess's teachers agreed that he was an incorrigible, and placed him in a class for those with behavioral problems. Had they known that he had begun secret preparations to change *their* behavior, they would have been shocked.

His math teacher was one of the first to encounter his new technique. Jess asked for help with a problem, and when she had finished her explanation, he looked her in the eye and said, "You really help me learn when you're nice to me." The startled teacher groped for words, and then said, "You caught on quickly." Jess smiled, "It makes me feel good when you praise me." Suddenly Jess was consistently making such statements to all of his teachers. And he would come to class early or stay late to chat with them.

Some teachers gave credit for Jess's dramatic turnaround to a special teacher and his rather mysterious class. They naturally assumed that he had done something to change Jess and his "incorrigible" classmates.

Rather than change them, the teacher had trained the students to become behavior engineers. Their parents, teachers and peers

... had become their clients (Gray, Graubard, and Rosenberg, 1974, pp. 43, 44).

The miraculous change in Jess's school behavior and the unbelievable improvement in his relationships with his teachers are just two examples of the effectiveness of behavior modification procedures in teaching learning-appropriate behavior.

In this chapter we will describe the steps in creating a tailor-made system for reducing problems in your own classes; introduce you to a number of systems that have already been tested; and explain how behavior modification principles, along with other techniques, can be used to increase student self-control.

HOW CAN YOU TEACH LEARNING-APPROPRIATE BEHAVIOR?

Although behavior modification often has the image of a sinister exact, science that features brainwashing techniques, it is really only a more systematic way of improving what teachers have been doing all through history. In educational terms, it involves specifying objectives, measuring entering behavior, helping students understand, rewarding appropriate behavior, evaluating student progress, and improving your system when necessary.

Specify Behavioral Objectives

Behavioral psychologists insist that objectives must be described in terms of overt student actions that can be counted. This requires teachers to translate general aims, such as "politeness" into "says 'please' and 'thank you' when appropriate" or "raises hand before speaking in class." Some researchers call these *operational definitions.*

Janice Ahern had been driven up the wall by a class of eighth-graders who bubbled into English day after day from a gym class in which a volleyball tournament was in progress. Typically the loud and excited conversations went on for five or ten minutes before she could get them settled down to adverbs and participial phrases. Her objective was "Students will be sitting quietly in their own seats one minute after the last bell rings." With this kind of precision, she was ready for the next step in behavior modification.

Measure Entering Behavior

Another contribution of the behavioral psychologists is their insistence on baseline data. If you are trying to change your students' behavior, you should know how bad (or good) it was to begin with. Heartfelt allegations such as "They were *impossible* when I took over the class!" will not do.

Jack Bromley had a door problem in his self-contained classroom. For some reason that the custodian couldn't remedy, the air currents conspired to slam it resoundingly time after time unless students exercised exceptional care. As a result, the untimely blasts were destroying the learning atmosphere and turning Bromley into a nervous wreck.

In order to establish a baseline, Jack brought his golf counter to school and clicked off every slam for a week. He planned to continue the procedure as he and his students worked on their door-closing skills.

Teachers often skip the counting procedures because they seem too time-consuming, but marks on the seating chart or dots on 3 × 5 cards will be well worth the trouble when they begin to prove that your behavior modification program is working.

Help Students Understand

Although traditional behaviorists would leave this step out, cognitive behaviorists believe that for human subjects like your students, learning proceeds faster when they have a clear picture of what you want them to do and a meaningful explanation of the reasons behind the request.

Myra Carter rushed into my office, wringing her hands. "My experiment is ruined," she moaned, "the kids changed before I reinforced them." She then described her carefully planned system to keep her third-graders from slouching in their seats.

In gathering the baseline data for her study, she was putting a small dot by the appropriate name in her gradebook each time a child slipped down in a seat. By the end of the second day, the number of slouchings was nearly down to zero because the students caught on to the fact that sitting up straight was important to her. No further reinforcement was necessary.

Sometimes a clear understanding requires a demonstration. Psychologists call this *modeling*. Richard Degnon is a stickler for safety in his industrial technology classes. In order to prevent serious accidents with the power tools, he not only goes through every precaution with each tool, but also follows all rules scrupulously in his own work. He even illustrates what *not* to do and describes in gory detail some serious injuries caused by careless procedures.

Regardless of the horror stories you may have heard about students defying teachers, most pupils will do what you ask of them if it is clear and reasonable.

Reward Appropriate Behavior

The genius of behavior modification is in the seemingly obvious principle of *positive reinforcement*. Students learn to do things that pay off for them. Still, the admonition to "catch them being good" remains a bit startling, since we have focused for so long on deviant behavior.

Simply put, your job as a behavior modifier (teacher) is to organize your classroom procedures so that students are rewarded for acting in a learning-appropriate manner and *not* for misbehaving. Perhaps the most basic illustration is Grandma's rule (the Premack principle).

Grandma always says, "You must clean up your plate before you can have dessert." The effective teacher plans each lesson so that the necessary but mundane learning tasks (plain old food) must be finished before the more exciting activities (dessert) may be enjoyed. For younger students or longer lessons, several "food-dessert" sequences may be called for. When the class is looking forward to a highly enjoyable learning activity, the following statement has near-magic results: "I hope we can finish our spelling practice so we can play a game of word baseball before the bell."

A corollary of the reinforcement principle is *extinction*: behaviors that go unrewarded become less and less frequent. In addition to serving up fudge brownies at the opportune time, Grandma must also find a way to keep deviant hands out of the cookie jar. Herein lies a problem.

Class clowns (Damico and Purkey, 1978) and other valued members of the group often get their kicks out of peer applause. So ignoring (not reinforcing) inappropriate behavior only brings about extinction when the teacher's attention is the main reward. When a disruption is peer-rewarded, a system such as the principal game may help you marshall this group influence on your side. We will describe it later in some detail.

In general, group rewards can be used in two ways: to modify an individual's misbehavior or to change a group-centered disruption. To illustrate the first type, suppose Edgar has formed the annoying habit of appearing late for school day after day. His untimely entrance not only adds another disruption to the work of his classmates, but it also means that his teacher must go over all the material again just for him. (Perhaps this is his reward for being tardy.)

Edgar's teacher can make an open-and-aboveboard deal with the class (especially those who live near his house) to help Ed get to school on time. The payoff might be some coveted learning game to be played at the end of each day that Ed punches in on time. Research studies (Hayes, 1976) have shown that a system like this not only changes the student's annoying habit, but also can improve his or her sociometric position with peers. Suddenly this student has become the key to a pleasant interlude for the whole class.

As with almost any such system, there are a few precautions a teacher must take before offering such a group contract. Whatever the preferred behavior, it must be one that the student is capable of performing and one that is under his or her own control. If Edgar's tardiness is because of the failure of his parents' car, group pressure might only make things worse.

Most teachers feel better about rewarding groups for changing counterproductive *group* behavior. Janice Ahern's noisy English class might shape up in a hurry if she offered to play a hit record at the end of each period in which they were quiet and ready to work by one minute after the bell. She would quickly discover her students beginning to cue each other with "Shh! Shh!" and "Come on, be quiet!"

Thus far we have discussed only rewards as consequences. While we have discussed punishment in an earlier chapter, a number of behavior modification systems include the assessment of penalties for misbehavior. Two of these are *time out* and *response cost.*

Time out refers to any brief period of isolation during which a deviant student is prevented from enjoying the rewards of the classroom. The idea is that isolation is boring and makes a student more eager to enter into classroom affairs again. Whether the time-out place is in the classroom or elsewhere in the building, it should be drab, devoid of things to do (unless work is to be made up), and secluded from other people. Although not as austere, it is analogous to solitary confinement in prison. In order to make the procedure optimally effective, the errant student should know why she or he is being sent there and how long the penalty will last. Some teachers set kitchen timers and allow students to return to their seats when the timers ring. If you have the time, it's a good idea to ask a returning student if he or she knows what to do to avoid going back to "solitary."

A *response cost* is any fine that is levied on a misbehaving student. This usually involves the taking away of some potentially reinforcing items such as tokens, privileges, recess, grades, and so on. Its use has been widely studied (McLaughlin and Scott, 1976) and most of the evidence suggests that no undesirable side effects occur, as they may for corporal punishment. For the penalty to be most effective, a fined student should know exactly what behavior was unacceptable.

Evaluate Student Progress

In the same way that you provide evaluations of your students' academic work, so you must provide them with information about how they are doing (feedback) in their efforts to learn effective school behaviors. If you have been careful to define your objectives in terms of overt behavior and if you have found a way to count the behavior for your baseline data, most of the hard work has already been done. All that remains is to conduct a periodic recount and make the results known to your learners.

Jack Bromley recorded the number of door slams per day on a line graph, where everyone could see it. He made a sort of ritual out of the posting of the day's results. On days when the door closings had been poor, some class members would groan or hide their eyes. On days when almost everyone had remembered, the new low number was often applauded with gusto.

Improve Your System

Even the most deft researchers conduct pilot studies in order to try out and "debug" their behavior modification systems. If things are not going well, the plan may be inadequate at any or all of the steps. The following questions may help you locate the problems:

1. Am I clear about what behavior I want my students to perform?
2. Am I counting the actions in the same way that I established the baseline?
3. Are my students clear about what I expect of them? Do they buy my reasons for asking them to change?
4. Is my payoff schedule appropriate? Are the "wages" something they want? Is it too easy or too hard to earn a payoff?
5. Does everyone know how she or he is doing? Can each one see the progress or lack of it?

If you have involved your students in constructing the behavior modification system, you can discuss it with them. Glasser (1978) insists that students should always be included in constructing and improving a classroom management system.

WHAT ARE SOME SYSTEMS THAT HAVE ALREADY BEEN TESTED?

Although the best behavior modification plan may be one you have constructed to fit your own needs and problems, the literature abounds with research studies describing systems that have already been tried out on real students. We will describe some here, in hopes that you may find some that can be modified to fit your situation. It will become obvious that each one was the result of the six steps we have described.

The Daily Report Card

Dougherty and Dougherty (1977) worked out this simple system to increase the assignment-completion rate of schoolwork and homework and decrease the rate of "talking out" in a fourth-grade class. To establish a baseline for the latter, the teacher counted the number of talkouts during consecutive one-hour mathematics and reading periods. This was done for ten days. About a week before the experiment began, a letter was sent to the parents of each pupil. It described the daily report card and suggested that they review the marks with their child each day, emphasizing the good ratings first and then making their own suggestions on how he or she might improve the lower ratings.

The front of the report card had a place for the student's name, date, period, and teacher. It was divided into *Behavior, Homework,* and *Schoolwork* sections. Under each section were the numbers one to four. The back of the card provided the descriptions of the behaviors to be modified. Each student had a report card taped to his or her desk.

The class was told that they were going to get a report card score for talkouts. They discussed the matter with the teacher until they understood what was expected of them and why. At the end of each hour, the teacher marked each person's card by circling a four for no talkouts, a three for one talkout, a two for two infractions, and a one for more than two mistakes. Whenever a talkout occurred during class, the teacher merely labeled it verbally as she marked her record.

The marked cards were sent home daily for about a month. After that they were sent home on Fridays only but were still scored on a daily basis. Results showed rapid decreases in talking-out behavior.

The Principal Game

Darch and Thorpe (1977) invented this variation of the good behavior game (Barrish, Saunders, and Wolf, 1969) to increase the on-task performance of the ten most deviant students in a disruptive fourth-grade classroom. The class was taught by a 21-year-old student teacher in her last semester of college.

Although the baseline data was gathered by graduate students using a ten-second time sampling technique, it could have been done during the writing or reading portions of the class by counting off-task behaviors such as talking out, talking to classmates, playing with objects, being out of seat without permission, leaving the room, or fighting. The counting was all done during a social studies class that was held from 2:00–2:30 P.M. daily.

After the preliminary measurements were made, the teacher explained that the class wasn't working as hard as they should and that she had invented a game that would help them work harder in social studies. The following system was then described. Each of the five rows of students became a team. A bell (kitchen timer) rang about six times during social studies class. Each time the teacher looked to see whether the individuals of each team were working hard. ("Working hard" was carefully defined by describing the explicit on-task behaviors that were expected.) If each member of a team was following the rules, a point was marked on the chalkboard under the team's number. A team did not receive a point even if only one member was off-task when the bell sounded. But all teams won as long as they scored at least five points during the half hour. As announced, the school principal came in right after class, asked the winning teams to stand, and talked with them about their accomplishment.

The game caused a remarkable increase in hard work and of course a comparable decrease in disruptive behaviors. Another phase of the experiment gave points to individuals instead of groups, with the principal's attention still being used as a reward. This system also increased on-task behavior, but the effects were not as pronounced as the team approach.

The Workclock

Devine and Tomlinson (1976) tested a procedure for reducing the nonattending behaviors of several entire classes of third- and fourth-graders. After some observers established baseline counts of specific attending and nonattending behaviors, the class was told that they were going to use a special clock to help them improve their study habits and that they could earn some free-time periods each day. The system below was then explained in detail until all understood.

While the clock was a rather sophisticated device with a remote control switch, it was essentially an electric timer that could be stopped and started. At the beginning of each workclock period, the students were told the total amount of time available for that period and the amount of time it should take them to finish the assignment. This work time was usually 15 to 20 minutes less than the period time available.

After the clock was set for the number of minutes of work time, it was allowed to run as long as all the class members were: in their seats, talking only when called on, and attending to business. If anyone broke any of these rules, the clock was stopped until the student compiled with the rule. Then the timer was allowed to continue running until the work time ran out. Whatever period time was left after the workclock stopped was used as a free-time reward.

In addition to the workclock system, any person who caused the timer to be stopped was given a "strike." Anyone who got three strikes during a single period was immediately sent to a time-out chair for one minute. Anyone who continued to break a rule was given another strike each ten seconds. The workclock resumed while rule breakers were serving their times out. Each minute served in the time-out chair had to be made up by that student at the beginning of the free time period.

If a student had three times out in one period, refused to go to a stay in the time-out chair, or continued to be noisy in time out following one warning, the child was sent to the office for the remainder of the period, including the free time.

The workclock system was used during only one academic period each day. The periods were rotated so that they were all covered at least once in three to five days. Then the clock was gradually phased out, and free time was given for completing work. The teacher gave verbal praise to those who were attending to business but still gave strikes for disruptive behavior.

The percent of nonattending behavior was thus reduced dramatically, and there was a significant increase in the proportion of time spent attending to classwork.

Elftherios and his colleagues (1972) constructed an automated light display to help control the out-of-seat behavior of 22 first-graders. The experiment took place during a 30-minute class in which the teacher worked with a small reading group while all other students were supposed to do seat work.

For nine periods before the game machine system was instated, observers counted the number of times children got out of their seats. Then the teacher explained how the game worked. A horizontal row of eight lights was designed so that one more bulb was lit automatically every thirty seconds in which no out-of-seat behavior occurred. After all eight bulbs in the row were lit, one bulb in a vertical column came on. At this time the children once more began to earn lights in the horizontal row so that they could obtain another light in the vertical column.

During the time when the lights in the horizontal row were going on, any out-of-seat behavior resulted in all those lights being turned off. However, no vertical column lights were ever lost once they had been earned.

For each vertical column light earned by the end of the period, the class received two minutes of recess time. If all six vertical lights were earned, the children received a party with cookies and milk. During the baseline period there were 16.4 out-of-seat behaviors per minute. During the seven game machine days there was an average of less than one child out of his or her seat *each day*!

A Good Behavior Contract

White-Blackburn and her colleagues (1977) found a way to increase assignment completion and decrease the disruptive behavior of four sixth-graders. After measuring the levels of disruption and on-task behavior to establish the baseline data, the teacher negotiated a contract with each student. The youngsters were presented with two lists. One consisted of the desired behaviors and assignments, along with the rewards that could be earned for doing each. The second list contained disruptive behaviors, along with the penalties that would be imposed for each. Both rewards and penalties made use of facilities and privileges available in the classroom. The teacher encouraged each pupil to exercise self-control and earn a reward by being good and finishing the contract assignments.

After each fifteen-minute work period, the teacher determined whether a student had earned a choice of a reward or penalty, and the appropriate consequences were administered. All of the students showed a significant increase in their on-task behavior and assignment-completion rate. In addition, they all got higher grades and decreased their disruptive behavior. During the time when the good behavior contracts were used, the experimental students compiled academic and behavior records that compared favorably with several "model students" who had not received contracts.

A Token Economy

O'Leary and Becker (1967) describe a successful "token reinforcement" program that they set up in a third-grade "adjustment" class. The class was made up of 17 nine-year-old children who were placed in this class because of their disruptive antics in the regular classroom. According to reports, temper tantrums, crying, fighting, and uncontrolled laughter were all reasons for sending these children to the "adjustment" class.

Previous experience had convinced the psychologists that such standard school rewards as praise, teacher attention, or stars or grades would not work with this class. One of their regular teachers insisted that when she called them "bad," they seemed to take it as a compliment and stepped up their rate of deviancy. When she complimented them on having done something well, they seemed disappointed and made faces at each other.

Using carefully trained observers, O'Leary and Becker recorded the behavior of the eight most deviant children for four weeks in advance of the experimental treatment. These third-graders were observed while they were participating in three structured activities: group reading, arithmetic, and listening to records or stories. A partial list of the behaviors marked as deviant included pushing, answering without raising one's hand, chewing gum, eating, name-calling, and talking and making other disruptive noises.

The next step in this experiment was to institute a carefully planned system for decreasing the proportion of deviant behavior and increasing the relative frequency of acceptable classroom behavior. Six simple instructions were placed on the board at the beginning of each day of the first week. They were: In Seat, Face Front, Raise Hand, Working, Pay Attention, and Desk Clear. The point system was then carefully explained to the entire class.

The children were informed that they would receive a certain number of points in their book, depending on how well they followed the instructions on the board. These points could later be used to "buy" small prizes such as candy, pennants, comics, perfume, and kites. A large variety of these "backup reinforcers" made it more probable that every child could find something that he or she wished to spend points on.

At first, the points were given at the end of each lesson period about five times a day. Initially, the teacher didn't want to go along with the rating procedure, because she thought it would take up too much time. When she found that she could give out all the points in three minutes, she agreed to try it.

For the first three days, points could be exchanged for prizes immediately after the token periods. During the next four days the children had to save up points for two days before they could spend them. The number of saving days was gradually increased so that during the last twenty-four school days, the children had to save up points for four days before they were allowed to buy prizes.

In order to make traditional social rewards more useful, the teacher was trained to give praise that was associated with prizes. She would often say, "I am glad to see everyone turned around in their seats. That will help all of you get the prize you want." The teacher also was instructed to ignore the deviant behavior of one child while rewarding another close-by child for obeying the same rule.

While the teacher was marking the individual points in each child's book, the group was usually directed by an appointed classmate, who asked the individuals to read portions of a story that had been placed on the board. Group points were added to a thermometer chart in the back of the room, depending on how well the whole class behaved during the individual rating period. After a certain number of group points were accumulated, popsicles were given to all 17 children.

Expert observers once more recorded time samples of the same children's behavior during the two months when the point system was in effect. An unbelievably low 10 percent of the recorded behaviors were rated as deviant during that experimental period, while 76 percent had been observed during the base period before the treatment began.

In addition, as so little of the teacher's time was taken up with discipline, she was able to give each child much more individual attention and had time to correct papers so that they could be returned quickly. According to O'Leary and Becker, the learning situation was so vastly improved that some children who had not finished an assignment for two years began to get perfect papers for the first time.

Student Behavioral Engineers

We opened this chapter with the startling transformation of a so-called incorrigible named Jess. The behavior modification system behind that change (Farnum, Graubard, and Rosenberg, 1974) is equally fascinating. Jess was just one of seven "incorrigible" students who were chosen to be the first behavior engineers. Two were black, two were white, two were Chicanos, and all were between 12 and 15 years of age. During the experiment a special education teacher trained them for one 43-minute class period each day, and they spent the other two periods with their regular teachers.

To obtain the baseline data, each student was trained to record the number of positive and negative contacts she or he had with the teacher each period. This took longer than the experimenters planned because at first these seven students were unable to recognize positive teacher behavior when they saw it. After the baseline data had been gathered, the students were taught a number of rewards to use in changing their teachers' behavior. Smiling, making eye contact, sitting up straight, saying, "Aha! now I understand": all these were reinforcers given by the students after each positive contact by the teacher.

They also learned to praise their teachers at the appropriate times by saying, "I like to work in a room where the teacher is nice to kids." When their teachers made negative statements to them, they were taught to say, "It's hard for me to do good work when you're cross with me."

Each student continued to keep records on the positive and negative teacher contacts. (Teacher aides also kept records, so that accuracy could be checked.) When the results were put on a graph, they showed that during the five-week experiment, positive student-teacher contacts had quadrupled, whereas negative contacts had decreased to nearly one-third of the baseline rate. A more recent study (Polirstok and Greer, 1977) produced many of the same results.

HOW CAN YOU IMPROVE STUDENT SELF-CONTROL?

Thus far we have explored ways that teachers can set up systems that will result in higher frequencies of learning-appropriate behavior and lower frequencies of disruptive behavior. In almost every case the teacher's presence is mandatory if the system is to be successful. Each of the six steps we have described requires the teacher to take some action to assure optimal effectiveness.

But most of us would eagerly subscribe to the adage, "Good discipline must lead to self-discipline." Practically, this means that we would like our students to behave even when we are out of the room or absent altogether. We often refer to this as self-control. Kanfer (1970) insists that true self-control takes place only when (1) there is a high probability of misbehavior, and (2) the person follows the rules anyway. In other words, temptation must be present before self-control can be exerted.

In this section we will describe four methods that show promise in helping students strengthen their self-control: self-management, cognitive intervention, positive attribution, and punishment timing.

Teach Self-management

McLaughlin (1976) has reviewed over fifty studies dealing with self-control in the classroom. Each of these uses at least one of the following components: self-assessment, self-recording, self-determination of reinforcement, and self-administration of reinforcement. As you can see, these techniques might be classified as self-imposed behavior modification.

Self-assessment refers to looking at one's own behavior to find out exactly what is going on. Sharon was a junior in a teacher education program. To fulfill one of her assignments, she taught a lesson to a small group of her classmates while someone else videotaped the performance. Upon viewing the results, she was horrified at the number of times she brushed her long hair from her eyes.

One of the early steps in Glasser's (1969) reality therapy is also concerned with helping students become aware of the misbehavior that is getting them in trouble. A next step involves the evaluation of that behavior to see if it is worth the trouble it causes. In a way, both of these things must take place before misbehaving students can describe change objectives for themselves.

Self-recording is the self-management analog of gathering baseline data. Once a student has identified a behavior that she or he wishes to change, a count must be taken to see how often it occurs. Connie was a bit outraged when Ms. Dressler accused her of talking out whenever she pleased. After just three days of putting her own checks on a talk-out card, she admitted sheepishly, "Gee I didn't know I was *that* bad." Her self-control increased markedly during the next month. Kazdin (1974) has referred to this phenomenon as *reactivity*.

Self-determination of reinforcement occurs when a student chooses what reinforcers he or she should receive and the amount appropriate for following certain rules. Felixbrod and O'Leary (1974) described a system in which each of eight third-graders was allowed to decide how many points he or she would receive for each right answer in math. It was shown that they worked as many problems correctly as another matched group in which the number of points was decided by someone else. During five final sessions in which neither group was rewarded, the self-determined group maintained their correct-problem rate as well as the externally determined group.

Self-administration of reinforcement means that students dispense their own rewards (which may or may not have been self-determined) for following certain rules. McLaughlin and Malaby (1974) described a group of sixth-graders who had reached a 100 percent assignment-completion level under a classwide token system. During a self-control phase of the experiment, these pupils were allowed to award themselves privileges whenever they had completed their assignments. Not only were their high completion rates maintained during this time, but the rates persisted until the end of the school year (over 50 days) in three subject-matter areas.

McLaughlin (1976) concluded that although these self-management techniques can be effective by themselves, they work better when students have experienced standard behavior modification programs and then are switched over to self-management. He also found that students could be trained to accurately self-record their own behavior.

And so one way of helping students improve their self-control is to put them in charge of their own self-management programs. Although they will require some assistance in assessing, recording, and reinforcing themselves for improvements, such programs can become self-perpetuating, saving the teacher time and lowering the misbehavior rates perceptibly.

Introduce Cognitive Interventions

Pressley (1979) has summarized a large number of cognitive manipulations that have been shown to increase children's resistance to temptation. We shall describe five types: self-verbalization, external verbalization, affect manipulations, cognitive transformations, and manipulations of attention.

Self-verbalization strategies are those in which the teacher instructs children to say things to themselves that will help them obey a rule rather than succumb to temptation. In a series of investigations with preschool children (Mischel and Patterson, 1976, 1978; Patterson and Mischel, 1975, 1976) researchers discovered that instructing children to tell themselves temptation-inhibiting statements ("No, I am not going to bother the new hamster") or reward-oriented messages ("I want to draw some fun pictures and see the hamster later") were both effective in helping them refrain from misbehaving.

Resistance to temptation can also be strengthened by *external verbalizations*. This technique features a prohibition by the teacher, accompanied by a rationale for behaving properly. A simple one used with first-graders by Kanfer and Zich (1974) was, "If you do not turn around and look at the toys, you will be a very, very good boy (girl)." Parke (1977) found that when teachers gave a verbal rationale for punishment, it was much more effective in strengthening self-control. He also discovered that the effectiveness of certain types of rationales changes with age. Whereas statements that emphasize the physical consequences of misbehavior ("Don't play with the toys because they might break") increase self-control of students from preschool through adolescence, rationales that allude to the rights and feelings of others ("Don't bother that drawing; it belongs to Myra and she wouldn't like it") and those that are empathy-based ("I will feel bad if you cheat") become more effective as students get older. So whenever you must voice a prohibition to your students, make sure that it is accompanied by reasons that are appropriate for their developmental level.

Affect manipulations also influence self-control. After reviewing seven different studies of the phenomenon, Pressley (1979) concluded that if students are told to think "happy thoughts" during a period of temptation, their self-control in that situation will be significantly strengthened. "Sad thoughts" were found to produce the opposite effect. The fascinating truth seems to be that children can influence their own behaviors through the use of covert, emotion-filled cognitions, and teachers can elicit these helpful responses by merely instructing them to "think about fun things."

Student self-control can also be strengthened if teachers instruct them to make *cognitive transformations* of their temptations. In one experiment (Mischel and Baker, 1975) children were told that, although they could have a few marshmallows now, they could have twice as many if they waited alone in a room till the experimenter returned. The experimental group, who were instructed to think of marshmallows as clouds, moons, or balls, was able to wait much longer in the room than a control group, whose members weren't asked to make the transformation.

In another study (Patterson and Mischel, 1975) children were asked to pretend that there was a wall between them and a forbidden object. They also showed more self-control than similar subjects who were not exposed to those instructions. Cognitive transformation provides a technique in which creative teachers can make use of their students' imaginations to help them resist temptation.

In a way, all the cognitive interventions we have discussed thus far (except perhaps self-verbalization) could be interpreted as *manipula-*

tions of attention. In each case students are directed to pay attention to stimuli that are less tempting than the forbidden object. It should therefore come as no surprise that hiding a tempting object or directing students to pay attention to something else has been shown to increase their self-control. In an earlier chapter, we referred to the constructive effects of isolating students from distracting stimuli, including the intrusive behaviors of their classmates. It appears that attention is a robust variable in the classroom.

Although there is no evidence that the effects generalize, Pressley (1979) concludes that self-verbalization and attention training are also effective in helping children refrain from specific impulsive acts. Students were able to modify their own cognitive tempos after merely being told to do so.

Use Positive Attribution

It appears that when teachers tell their students that they have certain admirable traits, they attempt to live up to the image, at least for a time. Miller, Brickman, and Bolen (1975) report an investigation in which second- and fifth-graders were helped to refrain from littering by being told that they were neat and tidy. This attribution approach was much more effective than trying to persuade similar groups that they *should be* neat and tidy. The authors suggest that persuasion involves a negative attribution, that a person should be something that she or he is not, whereas the pure attribution approach is not so hampered. It is probable that the same mechanism is involved here that was basic to our discussion of external verbalization with rationales. If a student believes that she or he is a tidy person, that is a reason for not littering. Some more recent studies have produced similar findings (Grusec, et al., 1978; Jensen and Moore, 1977).

Use Punishment Properly

We have discussed punishment in great detail in another chapter, and its connection with self-control is well known. Parke (1977) has shown that punishment is most effective when it is carried out by someone you like, early in the sequence of misbehavior, at a moderately high intensity. As we have said earlier, the addition of a rationale for the action is probably more potent than any of the other three.

SUMMARY AND DISCUSSION

In this chapter we have discussed the use of behavior modification and the mechanisms of self-control to teach students learning-appropriate behavior and decrease the frequency of misbehavior in the classroom. Behavior modification techniques include the specifying of behavioral objectives, the measurement of entering behavior, helping students understand your objectives, rewarding appropriate behavior, evaluating your students' progress, and improving your system. Specifying and explaining objectives helps students to anticipate the need fulfillment that will follow the completion of their assignments. The system of rewards confirms their expectancy. A number of researched systems were described in order to demonstrate these principles and provide effective alternatives for teachers to use.

Experiments with self-control have provided a number of techniques for helping students resist temptation when the teacher is not present. These included the use of self-management, cognitive interventions, positive attribution, and punishment. Cognitive interventions influence arousal, so that student attention is shifted to nontempting objects or activities. Positive attributions influence student esteem needs. Acting in harmony with the positive statements of the teacher fulfills their needs to be worthy and good. Self-management and punishment have both been related to our motivational model elsewhere.

FEEDBACK QUIZ

1. Which of the following steps comes first in the process of modifying classroom behavior? (a) evaluate student progress, (b)

measure entering behavior, (c) reward appropriate behavior, (d) specify behavioral objectives.

2. Which of the following phrases is a near-synonym to *measure entering behavior*? (a) construct an operational definition, (b) gather baseline data, (c) supply constructive modeling, (d) supply frequent feedback.

3. Which of the following terms refers to fines that a teacher could levy for misbehaviors? (a) extinction, (b) Premack principle, (c) response cost, (d) time out.

4. Which of the following procedures features a medium of exchange between preferred behaviors and positive reinforcers? (a) establishing a token economy, (b) ignoring student misbehavior, (c) providing a time-out room, (d) training student behavioral engineers.

5. Which of the following *is not* a component of a self-control situation? (a) high temptation, (b) low temptation, (c) rule following, (d) none are components.

6. Which of the four components of self-management is most closely related to the *objectives* step in behavior modification? (a) self-administration of reinforcement, (b) self-assessment, (c) self-determination of reinforcement, (d) self-recording.

7. Which of the following varieties of cognitive intervention features the students' pretending that tempting objects are something else? (a) affect manipulation, (b) cognitive transformation, (c) external verbalization, (d) self-verbalization.

8. Compared to *positive attribution*, persuasion is a less effective technique because it (a) contains a negative attribution, (b) implies future punishment, (c) relies on a rationale, (d) violates Grandma's rule.

9. Which of the following is the most effective time to punish a student? (a) before the misbehavior, (b) as the misbehavior begins, (c) in the middle of the misbehavior, (d) after the misbehavior is over.

10. Which of the following components of punishment has the strongest influence on self-control? (a) intensity of punishment, (b) rationale, (c) relationship between punisher and punished, (d) timing.

11. In behavior modification, making objectives clear and meaningful to students affects their (a) arousal, (b) expectancy, (c) needs, (d) reward.

12. Almost all the cognitive interventions may be described as manipulations of attention. Their major effect therefore is on student (a) arousal, (b) expectancy, (c) needs, (d) reward.
13. Positive attribution activates a student's _____ needs. (a) belonging, (b) esteem, (c) safety, (d) survival.

Nine

Discipline and the Exceptional Student

OBJECTIVES

1. Define *exceptional student* and list the three categories discussed.

2. List three general characteristics of students who are mildly mentally retarded.

3. Describe three general procedures that are recommended for maintaining good discipline with mentally retarded students.

4. List three symptoms that often appear in students who are learning-disabled. Explain why they are no longer thought to be "brain injured."

5. Describe three general procedures that are recommended for maintaining discipline with learning-disabled students. Explain why they are not effective "across the board."

6. List four points of view from which behavior-disordered students have been treated.

7. List four types of medical treatment that have been used to improve the behavior of behavior-disordered youngsters.

8. List five rules derived from the motivation model that are recommended for maintaining discipline with behavior-disordered students. Indicate the motivation component from which each is derived.

9. Explain why behavior modification is often effective in maintaining discipline with behavior-disordered students.

10. Explain what is meant by *interagent harmony* in the treatment of behavior-disordered students.

Zimmerman and Zimmerman (1962) describe an emotionally upset lad of eleven who threw a kicking and screaming tantrum several times a week. Whenever he was brought to his classroom, he would throw himself down in front of the door and begin the histrionics. This usually drew a crowd of staff members, who stood around him to witness the spectacle and comment on the probable causes of his misbehavior.

The teacher, sensing that the crowding around of staff members might be rewarding the tantrum behavior, had the lad brought into the classroom and placed in his seat. Although the boy kept kicking and screaming, his teacher went about her own work, ignoring his outbursts. After two or three minutes, his tantrum had subsided, and the youngster looked up at his teacher.

Taking advantage of his momentary attentiveness, his teacher told him that she would begin his lesson whenever he was ready. At this, the distraught lad began to cry and scream again. This outburst lasted for about five minutes. Then he sat up and said he was ready to begin.

His teacher immediately looked up at him and smiled. She walked over to his desk and said, "Good, now let's get to work." For the rest of that class period, this eleven-year-old worked quietly and cooperatively at his lessons.

During the days that followed, this teacher stuck to a well-planned system of withholding and giving reinforcement. Whenever her unruly pupil threw another tantrum, she assiduously ignored him. Whenever he quieted down, she came over closer to him, talked with him, or began an activity that she knew he liked. After several weeks under the new system, the boy's classroom tantrums stopped altogether.

Although his tantrums had been eliminated, this youngster continued to do other things that upset the learning situation. Not only did he use baby talk in class, but he constantly broke in with completely irrelevant comments and questions.

Following the same system that had vanquished the tantrums, his teacher paid absolutely no attention to either the baby talk or his inappropriate comments and questions. But whenever the lad was working quietly or making an acceptable contribution to class, she would talk with him pleasantly or ask him a question she was sure he could answer.

As with the tantrums, this lad's disruptive verbal behavior almost completely disappeared. He was able to work more efficiently in his classroom and was making good progress at the end of the study.

WHICH STUDENTS ARE EXCEPTIONAL?

You will quickly recognize that the Zimmermans were reporting the successful use of behavior modification techniques to decrease a series of disruptive behaviors. The report also makes it clear that this eleven-year-old was an exceptional student, one whose "uniqueness . . . requires an adaptation of the regular school program in order to maximize his or her functioning level" (Hewett and Forness, 1977, p. 75).

In this chapter we shall follow the lead of Hewett and Watson (1979) and deal with only three types of handicapped students: the mildly mentally retarded, the behavior-disordered, and the learning-disabled. With new laws mandating the mainstreaming of such students, regular classroom teachers will be called on to help them learn effective classroom behaviors.

WHAT TECHNIQUES ASSIST THE MENTALLY RETARDED?

Hewett and Forness (1977) point out that mental retardates have difficulty telling one stimulus from another and remembering what they have learned. They have often been severely deprived of multisensory experiences and are highly susceptible to the influence of others. As in the case of most handicapped children, these students don't require so much a different approach as they do an intensification of the techniques we have recommended for their classmates.

Make Rules Exceptionally Clear

For these students a short list of rules casually explained will not be enough. They must hear them, read them, see them performed, and practice them so that they are clearly perceived in terms of the specific behaviors they call for.

Increase Rewarded Practice

Because mildly retarded students often remember their mistakes instead of their successes, they need to practice the preferred behaviors many times in different contexts at spaced intervals during the day. Teachers must also be especially careful to monitor their behavior so that misbehaviors can be stopped before they are completed. Rewards for proper behavior should be immediate but not limited to social praise.

Teach Internality

Zigler (1961) has suggested that mentally retarded children must become more inner directed if their cognitive development is to be advanced. Therefore they must be helped to attribute their successes to their own effort ("That's a good job; I know you worked hard at it") and their failures to lack of it ("Sorry you didn't do so well; you'll just have to spend more time on it"). One of the reasons why behavior modification is so effective may lie in the fact that class activities are engineered to make sure that what you do determines what you get.

A mastery system of assignments is another way to teach internality. If a student is given several chances to correct and improve an assignment until it meets minimum specifications, she or he may learn that extra effort pays off and that academic achievement is not a function of luck or other outside forces.

WHAT TECHNIQUES ARE APPROPRIATE FOR LEARNING-DISABLED STUDENTS?

According to Hewett and Watson (1979), youngsters assigned to this category were once thought to be "brain injured." They are sometimes said to have "minimal brain dysfunction" or "minimal neurological impairment." Since doctors were often unable to confirm any neurological damage, they have shifted their attention away from the medical causes and are now concentrating on educational solutions to their problems.

Some Benefit from Medication

Although there is a wide variation of symptoms among these students, many of them are hyperactive; they are highly distractible and have severe perceptual problems. While the prescription of amphetamines has a calming effect on some of these students, they still have to learn appropriate school behavior like their nonhandicapped classmates.

Some Need Stimulus Limitation

Although strict elimination of extraneous stimuli seems to improve the learning success of some of these individuals, research has not documented its success across the board.

Some Must Have Perceptual Training

Students with visual-motor perception problems have been given special training in these basic skills. Although student performance improved on tests of perception, the gains did not extend to academic skills such as reading (Bryan and Bryan, 1975). The same fate befell efforts to train students in specific perceptual weaknesses revealed by the Illinois Test of Psycholinguistic Ability.

Each Needs Individualized Help

Hewett and Watson (1979) conclude that educators must match techniques with individuals, since there seem to be no specialized procedures that can be applied to all learning-disabled children.

HOW SHOULD BEHAVIOR-DISORDERED STUDENTS BE DISCIPLINED?

The student described by the Zimmermans at the beginning of this chapter may be categorized as behavior-disordered. They have often been called emotionally maladjusted. Hewett and Watson (1979) summarize recommendations based on four different points of view: biophysical, psychodynamic, behavioral, and ecological.

Some Need Medical Treatment

In severe cases, behavior-disordered students have been treated with tranquilizers, electric shock, and vitamins. Although you may have some children in your classroom who are on medication, you can do little more than remind them to follow their doctor's instructions. Experienced teachers report that they can tell immediately when some children have forgotten to take the proper dosages.

Although the classroom teacher should not be expected to give therapy to disturbed students, teaching in harmony with our motivational model will help many of these youngsters to improve both their academic achievement and their prosocial behavior. This is true for exceptional children in all other categories as well. A brief summary follows.

1. Use an interesting variety of approaches to teaching (arousal).
2. Let students know exactly what you want them to do and what rewards or punishments will result (expectancy).
3. Follow through with the rewards or punishments you promised (reward, punishment).
4. When punishment seems necessary, use response cost measures rather than physical or verbal swats (punishment).
5. Construct your learning activities so that students can fulfill their needs (needs).

Behavior Modification Is Effective

As we indicated in Chapter 8, there is overwhelming evidence that applying the principles of behavior modification can be extremely effective in maintaining classroom discipline. This is especially true for the behavior-disordered student. Such a well-structured environment that predictably and consistently rewards a youngster for learning and behaving appropriately may turn out to be the most satisfying place in that student's life.

Most of the systems that we described in Chapter 8 were constructed to give additional help to exceptional children who created discipline problems in the classroom.

Interagent Harmony Helps

In Hewett and Watson's (1979) description of the ecological approach to treating the behavior disordered, they refer to the necessity for cooperation among all of the agencies that impact the student. If the school, the home, and the social agencies can all agree on the rules, the student is immersed in a 24-hour therapeutic environment. It dispenses with the conflicting rulebooks and interagent inconsistencies that are stumbling blocks to improvement.

SUMMARY AND DISCUSSION

The exceptional student is one who must have some adaptation in the regular school program in order to achieve up to his or her capacity.

Mildly retarded youngsters must have rules made exceptionally clear; practice appropriate behaviors often, with appropriate rewards; and learn to feel more responsible for their successes and failures.

Since learning-disabled students vary so widely from one another, no single technique is effective across the board. Some benefit from medication; others must be protected from overstimulation; still others need specific perceptual training.

Behavior-disordered students have responded to medical treatment, psychotherapy, and especially behavior modification techniques. As with all other categories, teaching in harmony with the motivational model is beneficial. The greater the cooperation among the home, school, and social agencies, the more potent any therapeutic plan will be.

FEEDBACK QUIZ

1. Exceptional students all need (a) extra practice, (b) medication, (c) program adaptation, (d) psychotherapy.
2. Which of the following is a characteristic usually found in mildly retarded students? (a) difficulty in stimulus discrimination, (b) emotional maladjustment, (c) extreme distractibility, (d) injury to the nervous system.

3. Which of the following is recommended for improving the classroom behavior of mildly retarded students? (a) give perceptual training, (b) limit extraneous stimuli, (c) prescribe tranquilizers, (d) teach internality.

4. Which of the following is a symptom often associated with learning disabilities; (a) emotional maladjustment, (b) hyperactivity, (c) quick forgetting, (d) remembering failures.

5. Which of the following techniques has proven helpful in maintaining classroom discipline with learning-disabled students? (a) limiting of extraneous stimuli, (b) overlearning of rules, (c) psychotherapy, (d) teaching internality.

6. The medical treatment of students with behavior disorders represents the _____ point of view. (a) behavioral, (b) biophysical, (c) ecological, (d) psychodynamic.

7. Which of the following medical treatments has usually *not* been used to treat students with behavior disorders? (a) amphetamines, (b) electroshock, (c) tranquilizers, (d) vitamins.

8. In dealing with behavior-disordered students, teachers must use an interesting variety of approaches to teaching. This influences the _____ component of the motivation model. (a) arousal, (b) expectancy, (c) punishment, (d) reward.

9. Which method of handling behavior-disordered students features a carefully organized system of rewards and punishments? (a) behavior modification, (b) biophysical treatment, (c) psychotherapy, (d) the ecological approach.

10. Which approach for handling behavior-disordered students features special care to promote interagent harmony? (a) behavioral, (b) biophysical, (c) ecological, (d) psychodynamic.

References

Alschuler, A., et al. "Social Literacy: A Discipline Game Without Losers," *Phi Delta Kappan,* Vol. 58 (1977), pp. 606-609.

Arlin, M. "Teacher Transitions Can Disrupt Time Flow in Classrooms," *American Educational Research Journal,* Vol. 16, No. 1 (1979), pp. 42-56.

Aronfreed, J. "Aversive Control of Socialization," W. J. Arnold (ed.), *Nebraska Symposium on Motivation, 1968.* Lincoln: University of Nebraska Press, 1968.

Aronfreed, J., and R. Leff. *The Effects of Intensity of Punishment and Complexity of Discrimination upon the Learning of an Internalized Inhibition.* Unpublished manuscript, University of Pennsylvania, 1963.

Aronfreed, J., and A. Reber. "Internalized Behavioral Suppression and the Timing of Social Punishment," *Journal of Personality and Social Psychology,* Vol. 1 (1965), pp. 3-16.

Azrin, N. H. "Effects of Punishment Intensity During Variable-Interval Reinforcement," *Journal of Experimental Analysis of Behavior,* Vol. 3 (1960), pp. 123-142.

Azrin, N. H. "Punishment and Recovery During Fixed-Ratio Performance," *Journal of Experimental Analysis of Behavior,* Vol. 2 (1959), pp. 301-305.

Azrin, N. H., and W. C. Holz. "Punishment During Fixed-Interval Reinforcement," *Journal of Experimental Analysis of Behavior,* Vol. 4 (1961), pp. 343-347.

Barrish, H. H., M. Saunders, and M. M. Wolf. "Good Behavior Game:

Effects of Individual Contingencies for Group Consequences on Disruptive Behavior in a Classroom," *Journal of Applied Behavior Analysis*, Vol. 2 (1969), pp. 119-124.

Bar-Tal, D., "Attributional Analysis of Achievement-Related Behavior," *Review of Educational Research*, Vol. 48, No. 2 (Spring 1978), pp. 259-271.

Bloom, B. S., *Taxonomy of Educational Objectives Handbook I: Cognitive Domain.* New York: Longmans, Green and Co., 1956.

Brophy, J. E., and J. G. Putnam. "Classroom Management in the Elementary Grades," D. L. Duke (ed.) *Classroom Management, NSSE Yearbook II,* Chicago: University of Chicago Press, 1979, pp. 182-216.

Bryan, T., and J. H. Bryan. *Understanding Learning Disabilities,* Port Washington, New York: Alfred Publishing Co., 1975.

Cellar, S. "Practices Associated with Effective Discipline," *Journal of Experimental Education,* Vol. 19 (1951), pp. 333-358.

Cheyne, J. A., and R. H. Walters. "Intensity of Punishment, Timing of Punishment and Cognitive Structure as Determinants of Response Inhibition," *Journal of Experimental Child Psychology,* Vol. 7 (1969), pp. 231-244.

Church, R. M. "The Varied Effects of Punishment on Behavior," *Psychological Review,* Vol. 70 (1963), pp. 369-402.

Conger, J. J. *Adolescence and Youth: Psychological Development in a Changing World.* New York: Harper & Row, 1973.

Crispin, D. "Discipline Behaviors of Different Teachers," unpublished paper read at AERA, Chicago, 1966.

Cronbach, L. J. *Educational Psychology,* 3rd Ed. New York: Harcourt Brace Jovanovich, 1977.

Damico, S. B., and W. W. Purkey. "Class Clowns: A Study of Middle School Students," *American Educational Research Journal,* Vol. 15, No. 3 (1978), pp. 391-398.

Darch, C. B., and H. W. Thorpe. "The Principal Game: A Group Consequence Procedure to Increase Classroom On-Task Behavior," *Psychology in the Schools,* Vol. 14, No. 3 (July 1977), pp. 341-347.

Deut, J. L., and R. D. Parke. "The Effects of Inconsistent Punishment on Aggression in Children," *Developmental Psychology,* Vol. 2 (1970), pp. 403-411.

Devine, V. T., and J. R. Tomlinson. "The 'Workclock': An Alternative to Token Economies in the Management of Classroom Behaviors," *Psychology in the Schools,* Vol. 13, No. 2 (April 1976), pp. 163-170.

DeVries, D. L., and R. E. Slavin. "Teams-Games-Tournament: A

Final Report on the Research," *Center for Social Organization of Schools Report*, No. 217, Johns Hopkins University, August 1976.

Diebert, J. P., and W. K. Hoy. "Custodial High Schools and Self-Actualization of Students," *Educational Research Quarterly*, Vol. 2, No. 2 (1977), pp. 24-31.

Dollard, J., N. E. Miller, L. W. Doob, O. H. Mowrer, and R. R. Sears. *Frustration and Aggression*. New Haven: Yale University Press. 1939.

Dougherty, E. H., and A. Dougherty. "The Daily Report Card: A Simplified and Flexible Package for Classroom Behavior Management," *Psychology in the Schools*, Vol. 14, No. 2 (April 1977), pp. 191-195.

Doyle, W. "Are Students Behaving Worse Than They Used to Behave?" *Journal of Research and Development in Education*, Vol. 11, No. 4 (1978), pp. 3-16.

Doyle, W. "Making Managerial Decisions in Classrooms," D. L. Duke (ed.), *Classroom Management, NSSE Yearbook II*. Chicago: University of Chicago Press, 1979.

Duke, D. L., "How Administrators View the Crisis in School Discipline," *Phi Delta Kappan*, Vol. 59 (January 1978), pp. 325-330.

Duke, D. L. "Looking at the School as a Rule-Governed Organization," *Journal of Research and Development in Education*, Vol. 11, No. 4 (1978), pp. 116-126.

Duke, D. L. "Who Misbehaves?—A High School Studies Its Discipline Problems," *Educational Administration Quarterly*, Vol. 12 (1976), pp. 65-85.

Dunkin, M. J., and B. J. Biddle. *The Study of Teaching*. New York: Holt, Rinehart and Winston, 1974.

Eaves, J. "Reading Disability and Social Adjustment in Intelligent Children," *Educational Studies*, Vol. 4, No. 1 (March 1978), pp. 45-51.

Eleftherios, C. P., J. T. Shoudt, and H. R. Strang. "The Game Machine: A Technological Approach to Classroom Control," *Journal of School Psychology*, Vol. 10 (March 1972), pp. 55-60.

Felixbrod, J. J., and K. D. O'Leary. "Self-determination of Academic Standards by Children: Toward Freedom from External Control," *Journal of Educational Psychology*, Vol. 66 (1974), pp. 845-850.

Gagne, R. M. *The Conditions of Learning*, 3rd ed. New York: Holt, Rinehart and Winston, 1977.

Glasser, W. "Disorder in Our Schools: Causes and Remedies," *Phi Delta Kappan*, Vol. 59 (January 1978), pp. 331-333.

Glasser, W. *Schools Without Failure*. New York: Harper & Row, 1969.

Glasser, W. "Ten Steps to Good Discipline," *Today's Education*, Vol. 66 (November–December 1977), pp. 61–63.

Glickman, C. D., and C. H. Wolfgang. "Dealing with Student Misbehavior: An Electric Review," *Journal of Teacher Education*, Vol. 30, No. 3 (1979), pp. 7–13.

Glueck, S. and E. Glueck. *Unraveling Juvenile Delinquency*. Cambridge: Harvard University Press, 1950.

Gnagey, W. J. "Attitudes, Motives and Values of Facilitators and Inhibitors," paper read at AERA, Toronto, 1978.

Gnagey, W. J. "Effects on Classmates of a Deviant Student's Power and Response to a Teacher Exerted Control Technique," *Journal of Educational Psychology*, Vol. 51 (1960), pp. 1–9.

Gnagey, W. J. "Locus of Control, Motives and Crime Prevention Attitudes of Classroom Facilitators and Inhibitors," paper read at AERA, Boston, 1980.

Goldstein, J. M., and W. A. Weber. "Managerial Behaviors of Elementary School Teachers and Student On-Task Behavior," paper presented at AERA, San Francisco, April 1979.

Gray, F., P. S. Graubard, and H. Rosenberg. "Little Brother Is Changing You," *Psychology Today*, Vol. 7, No. 10 (March 1974), pp. 43–46.

Greene, J. E. "Alleged Misbehaviors Among Senior High School Students," *Journal of Social Psychology*, Vol. 58 (1962), pp. 371–82.

Grusec, J. E., L. Kuczynski, J. P. Rushton, and Z. M. Simutis. "Modeling, Direct Instructions, and Attributions: Effects on Altruism," *Developmental Psychology*, Vol. 14 (1978), pp. 51–57.

Hayes, L. A. "The Use of Group Contingencies for Behavioral Control: A Review," *Psychological Bulletin*, Vol. 83, No. 4 (July 1976), pp. 628–648.

Hewett, F. M. and S. R. Forness. *Education of Exceptional Learners*. Boston: Allyn and Bacon, 1977.

Hewett, F. M., and P. C. Watson. "Classroom Management and the Exceptional Learner," Duke, D. L. (ed.), *Classroom Management*. Chicago: University of Chicago Press, 1979.

Hillman, B. W. "The Family Constellation: A Clue to the Behavior of Elementary School Children," *Elementary School Guidance and Counseling*, Vol. 7 (1972), pp. 20–25.

James, H. W. "Punishments Recommended for School Offenses," *Elementary School Journal*, Vol. 29 (1928), pp. 129–131.

Jensen, R. E., and S. G. Moore. "The Effect of Attribute Statements on Cooperativeness and Competitiveness in School-Age Boys," *Child Development*, Vol. 48 (1977), pp. 305–307.

Johnson, D., and R. Johnson. "Instructional Goal Structure: Cooperative, Competitive, or Individualistic," *Review of Educational Research*, Vol. 49 (1974), pp. 213–240.

Jorgenson, G. W. "Relationship of Classroom Behavior to the Accuracy of the Match Between Material Difficulty and Student Ability," *Journal of Educational Psychology*, Vol. 69, No. 1 (February 1977) pp. 24–32.

Kagan, J. "The Concept of Identification," *Psychological Review*, Vol. 65 (1958), pp. 296–305.

Kanfer, F., and J. Zich. "Self-control Training: The Effect of External Control on Children's Resistance to Temptation," *Developmental Psychology*, Vol. 10 (1974), pp. 108–115.

Kanfer, F. H. "Self-regulation," C. Neuringer and J. L. Michael (eds.), *Behavior Modification in Clinical Psychology*. New York: Appleton-Century-Crofts, 1970.

Kazdin, A. E. "Self-monitoring and Behavior Change," M. J. Mahoney and C. E. Thorensen (eds.), *Self-control: Power to the Person*. Monterey, Cal.: Brooks/Cole, 1974.

Kounin, J. S. *Discipline and Group Management in Classrooms*. New York: Holt, Rinehart and Winston, 1970.

Kounin, J. S., and P. H. Doyle. "Degree of Continuity of a Lesson's Signal System and the Task Involvement of Children," *Journal of Educational Psychology*, Vol. 67 (April 1975), pp. 159–164.

Kounin, J. S., and P. V. Gump. "Signal Systems of Lesson Settings and the Task-Related Behavior of Preschool Children," *Journal of Educational Psychology*, Vol. 66 (August 1974), pp. 554–562.

Kounin, J. S., P. V. Gump, and J. Ryan. "Explorations in Classroom Management," *Journal of Teacher Education*, Vol. 12 (1961), pp. 235–246.

Kvareceus, W. C. *Juvenile Delinquency and the School.* New York: World Book Company, 1945.

Leffingwell, R. J. "Misbehavior in the Classroom: Anxiety, A Possible Cause," *Education*, Vol. 97, No. 4 (Summer 1977), pp. 360–363.

Lefkowitz, M., et al. "Environmental Variables as Predictors of Aggressive Behavior," *International Journal of Group Tensions*, Vol. 3 (1973), pp. 30–47.

Leifer, A. D., N. J. Gordon, and S. B. Graves. "Children's Television: More than Mere Entertainment," *Harvard Educational Review*, Vol. 44 (May 1974), pp. 213–245.

Lorber, N. M. "Inadequate Social Acceptance and Disruptive Classroom Behavior," *Journal of Educational Research*, Vol. 59 (1966), pp. 360–362.

Mager, R. F. *Preparing Instructional Objectives*. Belmont, Cal.: Fearon, 1962.

Marshall, E. *Caravan to Xanadu*. New York: Farrar, Straus and Young, 1953.

Maslow, A. H. *Motivation and Personality*. New York: Viking, 1954.

McCord, W., J. McCord, and A. Howard. "Familial Correlates of Aggression in Non-delinquent Male Children," *Journal of Abnormal and Social Psychology*, Vol. 62 (1961), pp. 79-93.

McGinnis, J. and G. Smitherman. "Sociolinguistic Conflict in the Schools," *Journal of Non-White Concerns in Personnel and Guidance*, Vol. 6, No. 2 (January 1978), pp. 87-95.

McLaughlin, T. F. "Self-Control in the Classroom," *Review of Educational Research*, Vol. 46, No. 4 (Fall 1976), pp. 631-663.

McLaughlin, T. F., and J. E. Malaby. "Increasing and Maintaining Assignment Completion with Teacher and Pupil Controlled Individual Contingency Programs: Three Case Studies," *Psychology*, Vol. 11, No. 3 (1974), pp. 45-51.

McLaughlin, T. F., and J. W. Scott. "The Use of Response Cost to Reduce Inappropriate Behavior in Educational Settings," *Corrective and Social Psychiatry and Journal of Behavioral Technology, Methods and Therapy*, Vol. 22, No. 2 (1976), pp. 32-34.

Miller, N. E. "Learning Resistance to Pain and Fear: Effects of Overlearning, Exposure, and Rewarded Exposure in Context," *Journal of Experimental Psychology*, Vol. 60 (1960), pp. 137-145.

Miller, R. L., P. Brickman, and D. Bolen. "Attribution Versus Persuasion as a Means for Modifying Behavior," *Journal of Personality and Social Psychology*, Vol. 31, No. 3 (March 1975), pp. 430-441.

Mischel, W., and N. Baker. "Cognitive Appraisals and Transformations in Delay Behavior," *Journal of Personality and Social Psychology*, Vol. 31 (1975), pp. 254-261.

Mischel, W., and C. J. Patterson. "Effective Plans for Self-Control in Children," W. A. Collins (ed.), *Minnesota Symposium on Child Psychology* (Vol. 11). Hillsdale, N.J.: Lawrence Erlbaum, 1978.

Mischel, W., and C. J. Patterson. "Substantive and Structural Elements of Effective Plans for Self-control," *Journal of Personality and Social Psychology*, Vol. 34 (1976), pp. 942-950.

O'Leary, K. D., and W. C. Becker. "Behavior Modification of an Adjustment Class: A Token Reinforcement Program," *Exceptional Children*, Vol. 33 (1967), pp. 637-642.

O'Leary, K. D., K. F. Kaufman, R. E. Kass, and E. S. Drabman. "The Effects of Loud and Soft Reprimands on the Behavior of Disruptive Students," *Exceptional Children*, Vol. 37 (1970), pp. 145-155.

Parke, R. D. "Effectiveness of Punishment as an Interaction of Intensity, Timing, Agent Nurturance and Cognitive Structuring," *Child Development,* Vol. 40 (1969), pp. 213-236.

Parke, R. D. "Punishment in Children: Effects, Side Effects, and Alternative Strategies," H. L. Hom and P. A. Robinson (eds.), *Psychological Processes in Early Education.* New York: Academic Press, 1977.

Parke, R. D., and J. L. Deur. "Schedule of Punishment and Inhibition of Aggression in Children," *Developmental Psychology,* Vol. 7 (1972), pp. 266-269.

Parke, R. D., and D. B. Sawin. *The Effects of Inter-agent Inconsistent Discipline on Aggression in Children.* Unpublished manuscript, Fels Research Institute, 1975.

Parke, R. D., and R. H. Walters. "Some Factors Determining the Efficacy of Punishment for Inducing Response Inhibition," *Monographs of Society and Research in Child Development,* Vol. 32, Serial No. 109 (1967).

Patterson, C. J., and W. Mischel. "Effects of Temptation-Inhibiting and Task-facilitating Plans on Self-control," *Journal of Personality and Social Psychology,* Vol. 33 (1976), pp. 209-217.

Patterson, C. J., and W. Mischel. "Plans to Resist Distraction," *Developmental Psychology,* Vol. 11 (1975), pp. 369-378.

Peck, R. F., and R. Hughes. "Social Adjustment and Achievement: A Cross National Survey," paper read at APA, New York, 1979.

Polirstok, S. R., and R. D. Greer. "Remediation of Mutually Aversive Interactions Between a Problem Student and Four Teachers by Training the Student in Reinforcement Techniques," *Journal of Applied Behavioral Analysis,* Vol. 10, No. 4 (Winter 1977), pp. 707-716.

Pressey, S. L., et al. *Life: A Psychological Survey.* New York: Harper and Brothers, 1939.

Pressley, M. "Increasing Children's Self-control Through Cognitive Interventions," *Review of Educational Research,* Vol. 49, No. 2 (Spring 1979), pp. 319-370.

Rafalides, M., and W. K. Hoy. "Student Sense of Alienation and Pupil Control Orientation of High Schools," *The High School Journal,* Vol. 55 (1971), pp. 101-111.

Raichle, D. R. "School Discipline and Corporal Punishment: An American Retrospect," *Interchange,* Vol. 8, Nos. 1-2 (1977-78), pp. 71-83.

Redd, W. H., E. K. Morris, and J. A. Martin. "Effects of Positive and Negative Adult-Child Interaction on Children's Social Preferences," *Journal of Experimental Child Psychology,* Vol. 19 (1975), pp. 153-164.

Redl, F. "Group Emotion and Leadership," *Psychiatry*, Vol. 4 (1942), pp. 513-596.

Redl, F., and W. Wattenberg. *Mental Hygiene in Teaching*. New York: Harcourt Brace Jovanovich, 1959.

Redl, F., and D. Wineman. *The Aggressive Child*. Glencoe, Ill.: Free Press, 1957.

Root, A. A. "What Instructors Say to Students Makes a Difference," *Engineering Education*, Vol. 61 (1970), 722-725.

Ryans, D. G. "A Study of Criterion Data," *Educational and Psychological Measurement*, Vol. 12 (1952), pp. 333-344.

Schrupp, M. H., and C. M. Gjerde. "Teacher Growth in Attitudes Toward Behavior Problems of Children," *Journal of Educational Psychology*, Vol. 44 (1953), pp. 203-214.

Searcy-Miller, M. L., E. L. Cowen, and D. L. Terrell. "School Adjustment Problems of Children from Small vs. Large Families," *Journal of Community Psychology*, Vol. 5, No. 4 (October 1977), pp. 319-324.

Sears, R. R., E. E. Maccoby, and H. Levin. *Patterns of Child Rearing*. Evanston, Ill.: Row Peterson, 1957.

Solomon, R. L. "Punishment," *American Psychologist*, Vol. 19 (1964), pp. 239-253.

Stouwie, R. J. "An Experimental Study of Adult Dominance and Warmth, Conflicting Verbal Instruction, and Children's Moral Behavior," *Child Development*, Vol. 43 (1972), pp. 959-972.

Thompson, G. G. "The Social and Emotional Development of Preschool Children Under Two Types of Educational Programs," *Psychological Monograph*, Vol. 56, No. 5 (1944).

Thurston, J. E., J. F. Feldhusen, and J. J. Benning. "A Longitudinal Study of Delinquency and Other Aspects of Children's Behavior," *International Journal of Criminology and Penology*, Vol. 1 (November 1973), pp. 341-351.

Walters, R. H., and R. D. Parke. "The Influence of Punishment and Related Disciplinary Techniques on the Social Behavior of Children: Theory and Empirical Findings," B. Maher (ed.), *Progress in Experimental Personality Research*, Vol. 4. New York: Academic Press, 1967, pp. 179-228.

Walters, R. H., R. D. Parke, and V. A. Cane. "Timing of Punishment and the Observation of Consequences to Others as Determinants of Response Inhibition," *Journal of Experimental Child Psychology*, Vol. 2 (1965), pp. 10-30.

Wegmann, R. G. "Classroom Discipline: An Exercise in Maintenance of Social Reality," *Sociology of Education*, Vol. 40 (January 1976), pp. 71-79.

White, R., and R. Lippitt. "Leader Behavior and Member Reaction in Three Social Climates," D. Cartwright and A. Zander (eds.), *Group Dynamics.* Evanston, Il.: Row Peterson, 1960, pp. 527-533.

White-Blackburn, G., S. Semb, and G. Semb. "The Effects of a Good-Behavior Contract on the Classroom Behaviors of Sixth-Grade Students," *Journal of Applied Behavior Analysis,* Vol. 10, No. 2 (Summer 1977), p. 312.

Willower, D. J., T. L. Eidell, and W. K. Hoy. *The School and Pupil Control Ideology.* University Park, Pa.: The Pennsylvania State University Press, 1973.

Yinger, R. J. *A Study of Teacher Planning: Description and Theory Development Using Ethnographic and Information Processing Methods.* Ph.D. dissertation, Michigan State University, 1977.

Zigler, E. F. "Social Deprivation and Rigidity in the Performance of Feebleminded Children," *Journal of Abnormal and Social Psychology,* Vol. 62, No. 2 (1961), pp. 413-421.

Zimmerman, E. H., and J. Zimmerman. "The Alteration of Behavior in a Special Classroom Situation," *Journal of the Experimental Analysis of Behavior,* Vol. 5 (1962), pp. 59-60.

Appendix

ANSWERS TO FEEDBACK QUIZZES

CHAPTER 2	CHAPTER 3	CHAPTER 4	CHAPTER 5
1. c	1. a	1. b	1. d
2. b	2. c	2. a	2. c
3. d	3. a	3. d	3. a
4. b	4. c	4. c	4. a
5. c	5. b	5. a	5. d
6. d	6. b	6. c	6. b
7. c	7. a	7. d	7. c
8. d	8. a	8. c	
9. c	9. b	9. a	
10. b	10. a	10. b	
11. d		11. c	
12. c		12. b	
13. a			
14. d			
15. a			

CHAPTER 6	CHAPTER 7	CHAPTER 8	CHAPTER 9
1. d	1. b	1. d	1. c
2. d	2. b	2. b	2. a
3. c	3. a	3. c	3. d
4. b	4. d	4. a	4. b
5. a	5. d	5. b	5. a
6. b	6. c	6. b	6. b
7. a	7. b	7. b	7. a
8. c	8. d	8. a	8. a
9. d	9. c	9. b	9. a
10. d	10. b	10. b	10. c
11. c	11. c	11. b	
12. c	12. d	12. a	
13. a	13. c	13. b	
14. a	14. a		
	15. a		

Index